POLLUTION AND THE
DEATH OF MAN

POLLUTION AND THE DEATH OF MAN

Francis A. Schaeffer

CROSSWAY BOOKS • WHEATON, ILLINOIS
A DIVISION OF GOOD NEWS PUBLISHERS

First printing, 1992

Printed in the United States of America

ISBN 0-89107-686-7

Library of Congress Number 92-74125

00		99		98		97		96		95		94		93		92
15	14	13	12	11	10	9	8	7	6	5	4	3	2	1

Contents

One

"What Have They Done to Our Fair Sister?"

S ome time ago when I was in Bermuda for a lecture, I was invited to visit the work of a young man well-known in the area of ecology. His name was David B. Wingate. He was especially known for his efforts to save the cahow bird from extinction. The cahow is a little larger than a pigeon and breeds only on a very few islands near Bermuda, just off the main island. Wingate struggled for many years to increase the number of these birds.

As we went around visiting the nests, we were talking together about the whole problem of ecology. He told me that he was losing ground in his battle, because the chicks were not hatching in the same proportion as before. If they had continued at the previous rate, he would have been well on his way to success. Instead, he found that fewer and fewer were hatching. What was the reason? To find out, he took an embryo chick from the egg and dissected it. Its tissues were found to be filled with DDT. Wingate was convinced that this accounted for the drop in the hatching rate.

The startling thing about this is that the cahow is a sea-feeding bird; it does not feed anywhere near land—only in the middle of the ocean. So it is obvious that it was not getting its DDT close to shore, but far out in the Atlantic. In other words, the use of DDT on land was polluting the whole area. It was coming down through the rivers, out into the ocean, and causing the death of sea-feeding birds.[1]

When Thor Heyerdahl made his famous voyage in the *Kon Tiki*, he was able to use the ocean water quite freely; but he later said when he tried to cross the Atlantic in a papyrus boat, the ocean water was unusable because of the large amount of rubbish.

A man in California very vividly pointed up this serious problem. He erected a tombstone at the ocean-side, and on it he has carved this epitaph:

The ocean born—[he gives hypothetical date]
The oceans died—A.D. 1979
The Lord gave; man hath taken away
Cursed be the name of man.

The simple fact is that if man is not able to solve his ecological problems, then man's resources are going to die. It is quite conceivable that man will be unable to fish the oceans as in the past, and that if the balance of the oceans is changed too much, man will even find himself without enough oxygen to breathe.

So the whole problem of ecology is dumped in this generation's lap. *Ecology* means "the study of the balance of living things in nature." But as the word is currently used, it means also the problem of the destruction man has brought upon nature. It is related to such factors as water pollution, destructive noise levels, and air pollution in the great cities of the world. We have been reading and hearing of this on every side from all over the world.

Near the end of his life, Darwin acknowledged several times in his writings that two things had become dull to him as he got older. The first was his joy in the arts and the second his joy in nature. This is very intriguing. Darwin offered his proposition that nature, including man, is based only on the impersonal plus time plus chance, and he had to acknowledge at the end of his life that it had had these adverse effects on him. I believe that what we are seeing today is the same loss of joy in our total culture as Darwin personally experienced—in the area of the arts and general life, and in the area of nature. The distressing thing about this is that orthodox Christians often really have had no better sense about these things than unbelievers. The death of "joy" in nature is leading to the death of nature itself.

In the 1960s and early 1970s when there was a profound interest in the philosophic basis for life and the problems of life, this sort of anxiety was even being expressed in the area of "pop" music. The Doors had a song called "Strange Days" in which they said:

> *What have they done to the earth?*
> *What have they done to our fair sister?*
> *Ravaged and plundered,*
> *And ripped her and bit her,*
> *Stuck her with knives in the side of the dawn,*
> *And tied her with fences and dragged her down.*[2]

At any rate, people everywhere began to discuss what could be done about it. An intriguing arti-

cle by Lynn White, Jr., on "The Historical Roots of
Our Ecologic Crisis" was published in *Science* mag-
azine.[3] White was a professor of history at the
University of California at Los Angeles.

In his article he argued that the crisis in ecology is Christianity's fault. It is a brilliant article in
which he argued that although we no longer are a
Christian world, but a post-Christian one, nevertheless we still retain a "Christian mentality" in the
area of ecology. He said Christianity presents a bad
view of nature, and so this is carried over into the
present-day post-Christian world. He based his
allegations of a "bad view of nature" on the fact that
Christianity taught that man had dominion over
nature and so man has treated nature in a destructive way. He saw that there is no solution to ecological problems—any more than there is to
sociological problems—without a "base." The base
of man's thinking must change.

In ecology in the 1980s there is not much writing or discussion on the basic philosophies underlying the consideration of ecology. This is parallel to
the lack of philosophic pornography, philosophic
drug taking, philosophic films, etc. However, in
ecology, as in these other areas, the thought-forms
of the 1980s were laid in the earlier period of the
1960s. At that time there was much serious consid-

eration, writing, discussion and expression concerning the worldviews underlying all these areas.

People are now functioning on the ideas formulated in that earlier period—even though those so functioning do not consciously realize it.

As Christians, we should know the roots in order to know why those who speak and act against Christianity are doing so, and in order to know the strength of the Christian answer in each area. If we do not do this, we have little understanding of what is occurring about us. We also do not know the strength of what, as Christians, we have to say across the whole spectrum of life.

The articles of Lynn White and Richard Means, from the later part of the 1960s are, I think, still the classic ones concerning the area of ecology.

Modern man's viewpoint in the post-Christian world (as I have dealt with in my previous writings) is without any categories, and without any base upon which to build. Lynn White understood the need of a base in the area of ecology. To quote him: "What people do about their ecology depends on what they think about themselves in relation to things around them. Human ecology is deeply conditioned by beliefs about our nature and our destiny—that is, by religion." Here I believe he is completely right. Men *do* what they *think*. Whatever their worldview is, this is the thing which will spill over into the external world. This is true in every area, in sociology, in psychology, in science and technology, as well as in the area of ecology.

White's solution was to ask, "Why don't we go back to St. Francis of Assisi?" He contrasts St. Francis with what he saw as the "orthodox view" of men having the "right" to despoil nature. "The greatest spiritual revolutionary in Western history, St. Francis proposed what he thought to be an alternative Christian view of nature in man's relationship to it. He tried to substitute the idea of the equality of all creatures, including men, for the idea of man's limitless rule of creation."

Both our present science and our present technology, according to White, are so tinctured with orthodox Christian arrogance toward nature that no solution for our problem of ecology can be expected from them alone. He said that technology is not going to solve the problem because it is powered with its view of dominion over nature, which equals limitless exploitation. "Since the roots of our trouble are so largely religious, the remedy must also be essentially religious, whether we call it that or not. We must rethink and refeel our nature and destiny. The profoundly religious, but heretical, sense of the primitive Franciscans for the spiritual autonomy of all parts of nature may point out a direction. I propose Francis as the patron saint for ecologists."

The discussion of this was picked up and carried further, and aroused much interest. In the *Saturday Review* of December 2, 1967,[4] Richard L. Means, who was associate professor of sociology at the College of Kalamazoo, Michigan, quoted White and extended White's concept and asked: "Why not begin to find a solution to this in the direction of Pantheism?" In fact, he tied this call for a solution based upon pantheism into what he called the "cool cats" of the generation in their interest in Zen Buddhism. He is saying here, "Wouldn't it be a solution if we just said, 'We're all of one essence'?"

So here pantheism is proposed as an answer to our ecological dilemma. But is it an answer at all? That is a question we must now consider.

Two

Pantheism: Man Is No More Than the Grass

Why not try to find a solution to this in the direction of pantheism? Here we find a use of the concept of pantheism by a Western scientist, a sociologist, in his effort to solve modern man's problem in relationship to the saving of nature—i.e., the ecological problem. This man seemed to be trying to use pantheism in a very specific way—not as a real, religious answer at all, but merely in a sociological or a scientific, pragmatic way.

Richard Means's article was entitled "Why Worry About Nature?" Means begins the article by quoting Albert Schweitzer: "The great fault of all ethics hitherto has been that they believed themselves to have to deal only with the relation of man to man." He thus quoted Schweitzer as saying ecology is a problem of ethics, but that man's only concept of ethics has been "man to man." Later Means said, "The notion that man's relation to nature is a moral one finds very few articulate champions, even among contemporary religious writers." He proceeded to refer to Harvey Cox's book, *The Secular City*. Cox, of course, is a very liberal theologian and at that time a proponent of the God-is-dead theology. Means said that even with Cox, "the city is taken for granted and the moral dimensions of Cox's analysis are limited to man's relations to man within this urban world, and not with the animals, the plants, the trees, and the air—that is, the natural habitat." It should be remembered that much modern theology is in the direction of pantheism, and thus Means' suggestion of a pragmatic pantheistic base for solving our ecological problems fits naturally into the climate which reaches all the way from the vague pantheism in much popular thinking today to the theological faculties.

Means went on to refer, interestingly enough, to Eric Hoffer, who was a popular American folk philosopher. He was a longshoreman who said many really profound things and had become very popular indeed with intellectuals. "Eric Hoffer, one of the few contemporary social critics who have met head-on the issue of man's relationship to nature, has warned in these pages of the danger of romanticizing nature" ("A Strategy for the War with Nature" in *Saturday Review*, February 5, 1966). Romanticizing means that one looks at nature and projects into it man's reaction. So one would look at a cat and think of it as though it were reacting as a man reacts. Hoffer very properly warned against this. However, his solution (according to Means) ends like this: "The great accomplishment of man is to transcend nature, to separate himself from the demands of instinct. Thus, according to Hoffer, a fundamental characteristic of man is to be found in his capacity to free himself from the restrictions of the physical and the biological." In other words, Hoffer was really not proposing that we should come to terms with nature (not as far as Means understood him anyway). What Hoffer was saying is that man has to transcend nature.

It should be said that it is correct to reject the romanticizing of nature as an answer or a solution. First, nature, as it now is, is not always benevolent; and second, to project our feelings and thoughts into a tree would mean that we would have no base upon which to justify cutting down and using the tree as a shelter for man.

Those who are familiar with Koestler's *The Man and The Machine* will recognize Hoffer's ideas to be merely a more poetic form of his concept. Koestler, along with Adler (*The Difference in Man and the Difference It Makes*) and Michael Polanyi of Oxford, attacks the classical view of evolution, at least pragmatically; these men were united as far as saying that it is leading us in the wrong direction. But Koestler in *The Man and The Machine* came up with the final solution by pleading with science to make a pill to bring together the upper and the lower brain. For Koestler, the lower brain deals with the instincts and the emotions, and the upper brain deals with the intellect and reasoning. According to Koestler, the real problem lies in the separation of the two. The point to be made here is that Hoffer's idea of man's "getting on top of" his nature in order to free himself from the restrictions of the physical and the biological is, interestingly enough, in the direction of Koestler's concept.

Reverting to Means' article, he went on to ask and answer an important question. Remembering that he was proposing the thesis that man's relationship to nature is a moral and not just a scientific crisis, his question and his immediate answer provide a brilliant snapshot of modern man: "What, then, is the moral crisis? It is, I think, a pragmatic problem."

Here was a remarkable combination of phrases; the moral dissolved into the pragmatic. He started off with a moral crisis, but suddenly all one is left with is a pragmatic problem. "It involves the actual social consequences of a myriad of unconnected acts. The crisis comes by combining the results of a mistreatment of our environment. It involves the negligence of a small businessman on the Kalamazoo River, the irresponsibility of a large corporation on Lake Erie, the impatient use of insecticides by a farmer in California, the stripping of land by Kentucky mine operators. Unfortunately there is a long history of unnecessary and tragic destruction of animal and natural resources on the face of this continent." Of course the pressure becomes greater on a world scale, and he was certainly right in pointing out that there is a serious problem. But that does not change his problem of dealing with the problem! He wanted a moral base on which to deal with the ecological problem, but soon all he had is the word *moral*. And what he was left with was the pragmatic and technological.

As one faces the growth of population, the ecological problem becomes even greater. In Switzerland, an excellent example was beautiful

Lake Geneva and the difference since we came to Switzerland thirty-two years ago—a major difference. Happily, the Swiss have, at great expense, begun to clear up Lake Geneva, but the growth of population on its shores required a major effort. Left to itself, the lake could not have cared for the population growth.

As the pressure gets greater worldwide, upon what basis, different from the one we have employed in the past, are we to treat the nature which is our environment and upon which our life in this world depends? As the Sierra Club calendar for 1970 put it, "The moon, Mars, Saturn . . . nice places to visit, but you wouldn't want to live there." Human life depends on the uniquely balanced environment of this world.

Means went on to talk about the passenger pigeons, of which there were once many in the United States; but they had become extinct. The same could be said about the seal industry. "The trouble is, however, we do not seem to learn very much from these sad happenings for (to the anguish of men who have thrilled to the images created by Herman Melville and the great white whale) such marine scientists as Scott McVay believe that commercial fishing is endangering the whale, the last abundant species in the world. For those more inclined towards the cash nexus, there goes a profitable industry." He continued that it is not only an economic loss, but that "for those of us who have a respect for nature—in particular, for our mammalian kinsmen—the death of these great creatures will leave a void in God's creation, and in the imagination of men for generations to come." The use of Means' phrase "in God's creation," which for many Christians would inspire hope as to the kind of answer he might give us, must not be misunderstood, as I will point out later.

Then Means touched on the other basic issues, referring to the mighty Hudson River and the Great Lakes and the state of the air we breathe. Because of these matters and hundreds like them we can see why men are wrestling, in a way that they have never wrestled before, with the problem of ecology. There is a true dilemma. Modern man has seen that we are upsetting the balance of nature and the problem is drastic and urgent. It is not just a matter of aesthetics, nor is the problem only future; the quality of life has already diminished for many modern men. For the future, many thinking men see the ecological threat as greater than that of nuclear warfare.

Means proceeded to offer his solutions to this dilemma. These were presented as first a negative, and then later a positive side. It is worth considering Means's thinking in detail, because it is representative of what, with various modifications, we have heard from a multitude of sources—and will be hearing in the next years. Indeed, Aldous Huxley, in his last novel, *Island*,[1] pictured a "utopian" future in which the first lessons given to schoolchildren will be in ecology. He then went on to observe: "Elementary ecology leads straight to elementary Buddhism."

There was a conference in Buck Hill Falls, Pennsylvania, called "The Conference on Environment and Population." There was a lightshow presenting the modern problems of ecology. Then the proposition was made that the answer must be in the direction of pantheism. We are going to hear more of this. Pantheism will be pressed as the only answer to ecological problems and will be one more influence in the West's becoming increasingly Eastern in its thinking.

What is man's relation to nature? Means asked, "Why is man's relation to nature a moral crisis? It is a moral crisis because it is a historical one involving man's history and culture, expressed at its roots by our religious and ethical view of nature—which have been relatively unquestioned in this context." Up to this point one could agree with his diagnosis. But then he went on to make a negative statement:

"The historian in medieval culture, Lynn White, Jr., brilliantly traced the origin and consequences of this expression in an insightful article in *Science* last March: 'The Historical Roots of Our Ecologic Crisis.' He argues that the Christian notion of a transcendent God, removed from nature and breaking into nature only through revelation, removed spirit from nature and allows, in an ideological sense, for an easy exploitation of nature.

"On the American scene the Calvinistic and the deistic concepts of God were peculiarly alike at this point. Both envisioned God as absolutely transcendent, apart from the world, isolated from nature and organic life. As to the contemporary implications of the dichotomy between spirit and nature Professor White says: 'To a Christian a tree can be no more than a physical fact. The whole concept of the sacred grove is alien to Christianity and to the ethos of the West. For nearly two millennia Christian missionaries have been chopping down sacred groves, which are idolatrous because they assume spirit in nature.'"

Means's answer to his question ("What is man's relation to nature?") must be found in his proposition that our ecological problem exists because of Christianity. He laid the blame squarely on Christianity as such, which has, in its intrinsic nature (on his premise), created and sustained the ecological problem.

In contrast to this, we can agree with the first part of the next paragraph in Means's article: "Perhaps, as Lynn White suggests, the persistence of this as a moral problem is illustrated in the protest of the contemporary generation of beats and hippies."

Our agreement with Means at this point centers on the fact that the hippies of the 1960s did understand something. They were right in fighting the plastic culture, and the church should have been fighting it too, a long, long time ago, before the counterculture ever came onto the scene. More than this, they were right in the fact that the plastic culture—modern man, the mechanistic worldview in university textbooks and in practice, the total threat of the machine, the establishment technology, the bourgeois upper middle-class—*is* poor in its sensitivity to nature. This is totally right. As a utopian group, the counterculture understands something very real, both as to the culture as a culture, but also as to the poverty of modern man's concept of nature and the way the machine is eating up nature on every side. At that point, I would side with the counterculture.

However, Means went on to suggest that the

hippies had what was perhaps a good solution. We may differ with him here, but undoubtedly he did understand what the counterculture's solution was. He says, "There may be a 'sound instinct' involved in the fact that some of these so-called beats have turned to Zen Buddhism. It may represent an overdue perception of the fact that we need to appreciate more fully the religious and moral dimensions of the relation between nature and the human spirit." This showed a quite proper discernment of the counterculture direction, which was, and is, toward pantheism. He would not need to limit it to Zen because it is pantheism in general. Thus, after having given a negative statement, saying we must get rid of Christianity, we have a suggested solution which is in the direction of the drift of our culture. For, as I have said, almost all the new theologians are drifting toward pantheism in company with the often present vague pantheism which comes in many forms today.

Much of the surrounding culture undoubtedly is moving in the direction of the West's becoming the East. And Means offered this solution with regard to the problem of ecology. This is undoubtedly why he quoted Schweitzer in the first sentence of his article. At the end of his life Schweitzer was a pantheist, laying great emphasis on "reverence for life," by which he meant: all that is is of one essence. Means started with Schweitzer as a man well-known in the West, but who was a pantheist.

This is why I questioned Means's statement about "God's creation." He is really using a Western term for a completely different concept. The term "God's creation" has no real place in pantheistic thinking. One simply does not have a *creation*, but only an extension of God's essence. In pantheistic thinking any such term as "God's creation"—as though He were a personal God who created, whose creation was external to Himself (all of which is wrapped up in our Western phrase "God's creation")—has no place.

It is clear that Means was talking about a real pantheism when he went on: "On the other hand, the refusal to connect the human spirit to nature may reflect the traditional thought patterns of Western society wherein nature is conceived to be a separate substance—a material—mechanical, and, in a metaphysical sense, irrelevant to man." What he was trying to do was link up the fact that all that is, is the same substance with nature. In this way he hoped to get a reverence for nature that would cause us to treat nature more gently.

He said toward the end of the article: "Such a view should help destroy egoistic, status politics, for it helps unmask the fact that other men's activities are not just private, inconsequential, and limited in themselves; their acts, mediated through changes in nature, affect my life, my children, and the generations to come."

What is interesting here is to see, as noted earlier, that his use of the word *moral* leaves us with only the pragmatic. The only reason we are called upon to treat nature well is because of its effects on man and our children and the generations to come. So in reality, in spite of all Means's words, man is left with a completely egoistic position in regard to nature. No reason is given—moral or logical—for regarding nature as something in itself. We are left with a purely pragmatic issue.

Means ended his article: ". . . Our contemporary moral crisis, then, goes much deeper than questions of political power and law, of urban riots and slums. It may, at least in part, reflect American society's almost utter disregard for the value of nature." Here we must agree with him. We have mistreated nature—not just the Americans, but other people throughout the world.

But notice—he gave no answer; and the "no-answer" falls into three different levels. First of all, the moral only equals the pragmatic, and this, of course, is related to the fact that a modern man in this position has no basis for morals because he has no absolutes to which to appeal. One can have a basis for something else—a social contract, a hedonism—but one can never have real morals without absolutes. We may call them morals, but it always ends up as "I like," or social contract, neither of which are morals. The latter is a majority vote, or the arbitrary absolutes of an elite in society, by which one can decide anything. And having no absolutes, modern man has no categories. One cannot have real answers without categories, and these men can have no categories beyond pragmatic, technological ones.

This can be seen in Means's article when he talks about cutting down the sacred groves. He has no categories whereby he could cut down a sacred grove when it is an idol and yet not be against trees as trees. As far as he is concerned, these categories do not exist. For him, the fact that a Christian would cut down a sacred grove when it has become an idol proves that Christians are against trees. It is rather like arguing concerning the Bible and art. The Bible is not "against" art. But supposing somebody argues that the Jews broke the brazen serpent which Moses had made (2 Kings 18:4). Here one has a serpent made of brass which the godly king broke; therefore, God is "against" art. Of course, from the Biblical viewpoint, it is not a statement against art at all. They were against the brazen serpent, which God had originally commanded to be made, *only when it became an idol.* God commanded this work of art to be made, but when it became an idol it was to be destroyed. This means that one has categories.

In contrast, modern man has no categories. This brings us back to the first point. The moral equals the pragmatic on a very crude level, in spite of all this nice terminology. So we must not think that Means (and other people like him) is a man giving a moral answer, a higher answer; he is not. It is a very low answer indeed.

The second thing is that Means uses these religious words (*moral* for *pragmatic*) over and over again as religious connotation words for the purpose of motivation. He is also using the word *pantheism* as a motivation word. This is something we must always be careful of. Words have two meanings, the definition and the connotation. The connotation goes on no matter what you do with the definition. Modern man destroys the definition of religious words, but nevertheless likes to cash in on their connotation/motivation force. This is precisely what Means was doing. By using these words, he hoped (even though he has indicated in his definition that *moral* equals *pragmatic*) that people would treat nature a little better because of the religious connotations of the words. It is one more illustration of a type of manipulation that is all about us.

The third thing to notice is that what one had was sociological religion and sociological science. It is important to note that Means was a sociologist. One does not have religion as religion; nor does one have science as science. What one has is both religion and science being used and manipulated for sociological purposes.

Edmund Leach, the Cambridge anthropologist, in an article in the *New York Review of Books* (February 1966), chose a certain scientific solution, not because it had anything to do with objective science, but very clearly because it led to the sociological answer that he wanted. Edmund Leach was at this point the very opposite of a scientist. Here was a scientist using science for sociological manipulation. With this, then, a parallel can be found between Edmund Leach in his article and Richard Means in his. The latter was also using science and religion for purely sociological ends. With it, science dies, religion dies, and all you have left is sociological manipulation.

Remember what I have emphasized before—it is worth considering this article by Richard Means in detail because the thoughts presented in this article are representative of those which will be sounded by many voices, with a multitude of variations and subtleties. This is true about the theoretical and practical discussions in general, and the ecological discussion of the relationship of man to nature in particular. And the same basic factors are involved, whether the unity of everything that is is expressed with some form of the religious connotation word *pantheism*, or with purely secular terms, in reducing everything to energy particles.

Let us examine the reasons why pantheism in any form does not give a sufficient answer. Pantheism eventually gives no meaning to any particulars. In true pantheism unity has meaning, but the particulars have no meaning, including the particular of man. Also, if the particulars have no meaning, then nature has no meaning, including the particular of man. A meaning to particulars does not exist philosophically in any pantheistic system, whether it is the pantheism of the East or the "pan-everything-ism" in the West, beginning everything only with the energy particles. In both cases, eventually the particulars have no meaning. Pantheism gives you an answer for unity, but it gives no meaning to the diversity. Pantheism is not an answer.

This is not just a theoretical dilemma—that

the particulars have no meaning in pantheism. It is not just a vague philosophical objection. It leads to important conclusions. First, any "results" one does get from pantheism are obtained only by projecting *man's* feelings into *nature*. And that is simply the romanticism concerning which Hoffer warned, an endowing of the lower creation with a human reaction. So when we see a chicken, we endow its love-life with human qualities. But that is to evade the *reality* of the chicken. This kind of an answer can get results from these motivation words only by projecting human feelings into nature, and Hoffer was right to reject this.

What I am saying is that a pantheistic answer is not just a theoretically weak answer, but it is also a weak answer in *practice*. A man who begins to take a pantheistic view of nature has no answer for the fact that nature has two faces: it has a benevolent face, but it may also be an enemy. The pantheist views nature as normal. In this view, there is no place for abnormality in nature.

This was a very practical problem in Camus's *The Plague* where Camus comments on the dilemma facing Orion the recatcher: "Well, if he joins with the doctors and fights the plague, he is fighting against God, or if he joins with the priest and does not fight God by not fighting the plague, he is not being humanitarian." Camus never resolved this problem. If we accept this romantic and non-Christian mysticism, the difficulty is that we have no solution for the fact that nature is often not benevolent. If everything is one, and a part of one essence with no basic distinction, how does one explain nature when it is destructive? What is the theoretical answer? And as Camus understood, it isn't just a theoretical problem. Rather, how do I fight the plague?

The Christian *can* fight it. When Christ stood in front of the tomb of Lazarus (John 11), He was claiming to be divine and yet He was furious. The Greek makes it plain that He was *furious.* He could be furious with the plague *without being angry with Himself.* This turns upon the historic, space-time Fall. Consequently, the Christian does not have Camus's difficulty. But if one is putting forth a pantheistic, mystical answer, there is no solution to the fact that nature is not always benevolent. One has no way to understand the origin of this double fact of nature; one has no real way to "fight the plague." There may be much high-sounding talk, but eventually this is true of all pantheism, either Eastern or modern Western—either any of the vague forms of pantheism which are all about us or the modern theologian.

Again, a pantheistic stand always brings man to an impersonal and low place rather than elevating him. This is an absolute rule. Whether the pantheistic answer is the modern scientism which relates everything back to the energy particle, or whether it is Eastern, eventually nature does not become high, but man becomes low. This can be seen over and over again. Schweitzer spoke much of reverence for life, but a doctor who worked with him said that he wished Schweitzer had had less reverence for life and more love for it and for people. At the end of his life Schweitzer's pantheism, instead of going toward a higher view of those among whom he worked, went toward a lower view.

The Eastern pantheism leads to this same thing. In the Eastern countries there is no real base for the dignity of man. Thus, it must be pointed out that *idealistic* Marxism could only have come as a Christian heresy; it could never have originated in the East, because there is no place for a genuine dignity of man in the pantheistic East. Idealistic Marxism is a Judeo-Christian heresy.

The same is true even in the realm of economics. The economic dilemma of India is complicated by their pantheistic system in which the rats and cows are allowed to eat up food that the people need. Instead of man being raised, in reality he is lowered. The rats and cows are finally given preference to man himself, and man begins to disappear into the woodwork in economics as well as in the area of personality and love.[2]

Those who propose the pantheistic answer ignore this fact—that far from raising nature to man's height, pantheism must push both man and nature down into a bog. Without categories, there is eventually no reason to distinguish bad nature from good nature. Pantheism leaves us with the Marquis de Sade's dictum, "What is, is right" in morals, and man becomes no more than the grass.

Three

Other Inadequate Answers

P antheism is not the answer. If the West turns to pantheism to solve its ecological problems, the human will be even more reduced, and impersonal technology will reign even more securely. But having said that, let us quickly add that a poor Christianity is not the answer either. There is a "Christianity" which gives no better answer than pantheism: Byzantine, pre-Renaissance Christianity, for instance. This Byzantine concept was that the only truly valuable thing is heavenly— so high, so lifted up, so holy that only symbols were used. For example, they never painted a real picture of Mary; the icons and mosaics are only symbols of her. The only thing that really mattered in life was the heavenly. This kind of Christianity will never give an answer to the problem of nature, for in this view nature has no real importance. So there is indeed a form of Christianity that has no *proper* emphasis upon nature.

At a certain point in history, as the medieval died and Renaissance man was born, Van Eyck began to paint nature. Likewise, in the marvelous Carmine Chapel in Florence, Masaccio went beyond Giotto and began to paint nature as real nature. At that point they could have gone toward a truly Christian art, because there is a real place for nature in true Christianity. Those who followed Van Eyck and his backgrounds, and Masaccio painting in the round with the proper light and so on, could have gone either way—toward a truly Christian art, in which nature had a proper place, or toward humanism.

Pantheism is no answer for a proper view of nature, but one must understand that just any kind of Christianity is no answer either; not a Byzantine Christianity, nor a Christianity based on a nature/grace dichotomy. Neither will produce an answer. Nor is there any answer in the concept of nature and freedom held by Jean-Jacques Rousseau or Kant.[1] In all these areas one searches in vain for the Christian answer, or any real answer (even if Christian terms are used), and this includes any real answer for a proper view of nature.

But of course there exists a different kind of Christianity. The Christianity of the Reformation does give a unified answer, and this answer has meaning not only in speaking about heavenly things, but also about nature. God has spoken; and because of this, there is a unity. This gave the unity of the Reformation, in contrast to the nature/grace nonunity of the Renaissance. It turns upon the fact that God has spoken and told us something about both heavenly things and nature. On the basis of God's speaking, we know something truly of both universals and particulars, and this includes the meaning and proper use of the particulars.

This unity has not come from a rationalism, a humanism, in which man is generating something out of himself, gathering and looking at the particulars and then trying to make a universal, whether it be a philosophic universal, or Leonardo da Vinci trying to paint the "soul."[2] The Reformation believed what the Bible says: that God has revealed truth about Himself and the cosmos, and that therefore there is a unity. The Westminster Confession of Faith (of the seventeenth century) said that God has revealed His attributes, and these are true not only to us *but to Him*. We have a knowledge which is true both to us and to God. To us it is true but not exhaustive knowledge, as God is infinite and we are finite. But it is true, since God has spoken about Himself and about the cosmos and about history. This is the kind of Christianity that has an answer, including an answer about nature and man's relationship to it.

One feels this already in the paintings of Dürer, who in fact was painting a few years before Luther spoke out. As the late Professor Rookmaaker of the Free University in Amsterdam pointed out, Dürer went through a humanistic period, and then he rejected the humanistic answer and came up with the Biblical answer, and in that answer he knew what to do with nature.

One can also think of the post-Reformation Dutch painters, who painted nature beautifully and in its proper place. Without question, the greatest Dutch painting is that in which nature, the world as it is, had a tremendously important place. With the following of Van Eyck in the north (prior to the Reformation) and Masaccio in the south, Renaissance painting did not go in the right direction; it went into humanism that came to a dead end in modern man. Modern man does not have any answer for nature either in his painting or his use of nature in life—just as he does not have any answer for man. But the Dutch painters after the Reformation were able to give nature its proper place, the Reformation having restored a unity on the basis of the revelation of God.

It is well to stress, then, that Christianity does not automatically have an answer; it has to be the right kind of Christianity. Any Christianity that rests upon a dichotomy—some sort of Platonic concept—does not have an answer to nature; and we must say with sorrow that much orthodoxy, much evangelical Christianity, is rooted in a Platonic concept. In this kind of Christianity there is only interest in the "upper story," in the heavenly things—only in "saving the soul" and getting it to Heaven. In this Platonic concept, even though orthodox and evangelical terminology is used, there is little or no interest in the proper pleasure of the body or the proper uses of the intellect. In such a Christianity, there is a strong tendency to see nothing in nature beyond its use as one of the classic proofs of God's existence. "Look at nature," we are told; "look at the Alps. God must have made them." And that is the end. Nature has become merely an academic proof of the existence of the Creator, with little value in itself. Christians of this outlook do not show an interest in nature *itself.* They use it simply as an apologetic weapon, rather than thinking or talking about the real value of nature.

An extreme example of this attitude can be

found in what the Dutch Christians have called the Black Stocking Calvinists in Holland. These have a tradition that they may treat their animals cruelly because the animals do not have a soul and are not going to Heaven. They would claim to be very, very orthodox, but actually they are not orthodox. Theirs is Christianity in a perverted form. As far as creedalism is concerned, they may be very strong, but they will actually beat and kick their animals because in their view the animals do not have souls or a heavenly destiny. Thus they are not worthy of kind treatment. This is a sub-Christian view concerning nature.

One can find deficient concepts in less extreme forms in many places. Some years ago I was lecturing in a certain Christian school. Just across a ravine from the school there was what they called a "hippie community." On the far side of the ravine one saw trees and some farms. Here, I was told, they had pagan grape stomps. Being interested, I made my way across the ravine and met one of the leading men in this "Bohemian" community.

We got on very well as we talked of ecology, and I was able to speak of the Christian answer to life and ecology. He paid me the compliment (and I accepted it as such) of telling me that I was the first person from "across the ravine" who had ever been shown the place where they did, indeed, have grape stomps and to see the pagan image they had there. This image was the center of these rites. The whole thing was set against the classical background of Greece and Rome.

Having shown me all this, he looked across to the Christian school and said to me, "Look at that; isn't that ugly?" And it was! I could not deny it. It was an ugly building, without even trees around it.

It was then that I realized what a poor situation this was. When I stood on Christian ground and looked at the Bohemian people's place, it was beautiful. They had even gone to the trouble of running their electric cables under the level of the trees so that they couldn't be seen. Then I stood on pagan ground and looked at the Christian community and saw ugliness. Here you have a Christianity that is failing to take into account man's responsibility and proper relationship to nature.

So pantheism is not going to solve our international ecological problem. Lynn White's position is not going to solve it because it is obvious in practice that man really does have a special role in nature that nothing else has. And, third, a Platonic view of Christianity is not going to solve it. Here, unhappily, Lynn White is right. He looks back over the history of Christianity and sees that there is too much Platonic thinking in Christianity where nature is concerned.

Now, what is the genuine, Biblical view that *will* give a sufficient base for solving the ecological problem? What should be our attitude to and our treatment of nature? What is the Biblical view of nature? Let us now consider that question.

Four

The Christian View: Creation

The beginning of the Christian view of nature is the concept of creation: that God was there before the beginning of the space-time continuum and God created everything out of nothing. From this, we must understand that creation is not an extension of the essence of God. Created things have an objective existence in themselves. They are really there. .

Whitehead, Oppenheimer, and others have pointed out that modern science was only born out of a surrounding consensus of historic Christianity. Why? Because, as Whitehead has emphasized, Christianity believes that God has created an external world that is really there; and because He is a reasonable God, one can expect to be able to find the order of the universe *by reason*. Whitehead was absolutely right about this. He was not a Christian, but he understood that there would never have been modern science without the Biblical view of Christianity.

It is the same in the area of nature. It is the Biblical view of nature that gives nature a value *in itself*: not to be used merely as an argument in apologetics, but of value in itself because God made it.

Jean-Paul Sartre stated that the basic philosophic problem is that something exists. And nature *is* there—even if man doesn't know why. Christians know why it is there: because God created it out of nothing, and it is in its place! Created things are not an extension of God's essence. They are not a "dream of God," as some Eastern philosophies claim; they are really there. That may sound naive and obvious, but it is not; it is a profound concept with profound consequences. Think of Hume's arguments against cause and effect. They were demolished in Hume's day-by-day experience because nature is really there, and it exists because God made it to exist; and existing, the particulars of nature affect other particulars of nature which are there.

It is intriguing to note, as we did in the preceding chapter, that after the Reformation the Dutch painters began to paint nature, no longer feeling any necessity to restrict themselves to religious subjects. In fact, from that time on religious subjects were relatively rarely painted. Most artists had suddenly found that nature was worth painting, and that it is properly Christian to paint it.

Now it follows that if we return to the Reformation's Biblical view that nature is worth painting, so the nature which we paint is also worth something in itself. This is the true Christian mentality. It rests upon the reality of creation out of nothing by God. But it also follows that all things are equally created by God. All things were equally created out of nothing. *All things, including man, are equal in their origin*, as far as creation is concerned.

All of this depends, of course, on the nature of God. What kind of God exists? The Judeo-Christian God is different from all the other gods in the world. The Judeo-Christian God is the personal-infinite God. The gods of the East are infinite by definition, in that they contain everything including the male and female equally, the cruel and the noncruel equally, and so on. But they are not personal. In contrast, the gods of the West—the Greek and the Roman gods, the great god Thor and the Anglo-Saxon gods—were personal but were always limited and finite.

So the Judeo-Christian God is unique: He is infinite and He is, at the same time, personal.

Now how did He create? On the side of His infinity there is the great chasm. He creates all things, and He alone is Creator. Everything else is created. Only He is infinite, and only He is the Creator; everything else is dependent. So man, the animal, the flower, and the machine, in the Biblical viewpoint, are equally separated from God in that He created them all. On the side of infinity man is as separated from God as is the machine.

THE PERSONAL-INFINITE GOD

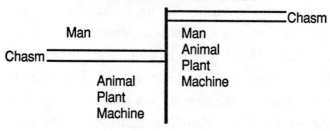

So on the side of the infinite the chasm is between God and everything else, between the Creator and all created things.

But there is another side—the personal. Here the animal, the flower, and the machine are below the chasm. On the side of God's infinity everything else is finite and equally separated from God; but on the side of His personality, God has created man in

His own image. Therefore, man's relationship is upward rather than downward—a tremendous factor that opens door after door for the comprehension of confused modern man.

Man is separated, as personal, from nature because he is made in the image of God. That is, he has personality, and as such he is unique in the creation; but he is united to all other creatures as being *created*. Man is separated from everything else, but that does not mean that there is not also a proper relationship downward on the side of man's being created and finite.

But his relationship is not *only* downward. Albert Schweitzer related himself to the hippopotamus coming through the bush, because Schweitzer had no sufficient relationship upward. But man is made in the image of God, who is personal; thus he has two relationships—upward and downward. Of course, if he does not find his relationship upward he will have to find this relationship (or integration point) downward. Christians reject this totally because we know who man is; we are not threatened by the machine as modern man is, because we know who we are. This is not said proudly, but humbly and reverently; we know we are made in the image of God. We reject an attitude that makes our integration point downward. Christians reject the view that there is no distinction—or only a quantitative distinction—between man and other things; *and* they reject the view that man is totally separated from all other things.

As a Christian I say, "Who am I?" Am I only the hydrogen atom, the energy particle extended? No, I am made in the image of God. I know who I am. Yet, on the other hand, when I turn around and I face nature, I face something that is like myself. I, too, am created, just as the animal and the plant and the atom are created.

There is a parallel here to our call to love. The Christian is told to love as brothers in Christ other Christians only. All men are not our brothers in Christ, as the liberal theologian would have us believe. From the Biblical point of view, brothers have the same father. Only when a man comes and casts himself upon the prophesied Messiah of the Old Testament as the Savior (for Christ has come in His substitutionary work) does God become his Father. This is clear from the teaching of Jesus. Therefore, not all men are our brothers in Christ.

However, just because the Bible says that not all men are our brothers, it does not follow that we are not to love *all* men as our neighbors. So one has the tremendous impact of the teaching of Jesus about the good Samaritan: I am to love on the basis of my neighborliness all that which is one blood with myself. And the New Testament uses that expression, "one blood," to indicate the unity of all people by God's creation. We are people who know we have one common origin with all races, all languages, and all people.

But only the Christian knows why he has a common origin. The evolutionist, the "modern" man, has no real reason to understand a common origin or a common relationship among men, except a biological one: people breed. That is all with which they are left.

The Christian, however, understands that people are all from one origin. We are all of one flesh; we are of one blood. One can say that from the Biblical viewpoint, there are *two* humanities: one, the humanity that stands in revolt against God, and the other, the humanity that used to be in revolt against God (because none of us came into this second humanity by natural birth). The members of this second group, having believed on Christ, have cast themselves upon God and have become the sons of God.

Yet one must never forget there is only one humanity, and this is no paradox. There are orthodox Christians who will not let it be said that there is only one humanity, because they so strongly reject the liberal emphasis upon the one humanity at the expense of justification, but this is shortsighted. There are two, but one. The Christian is called to understand that there are two humanities, and to love his brothers in Christ especially; and yet Christ also lays upon us the love of all men, as our neighbors, because we *are* one.

It is the same in regard to nature. On a very different level, we are separated from that which is the "lower" form of creation, yet we are united to it. One must not choose; one must say both. I am separated from it because I am made in the image of God; my integration point is upward, not downward; it is not turned back upon creation. Yet at the same time I am united to it because nature and man are both created by God.

This is a concept that no other philosophy has. Among other things, it explains the machine functions of man. For example, we have a common lung system with dogs and cats. This is not surprising. Both man and these other creatures have been created by God to fit a common environment. There is a common relationship in these mechanical functions, which relates man downward. There *are* machine functions to man. Psychologically there is a conditioning, not only in the animals but also, to a more limited extent, in man. This is to be expected, in view of our relationship both downward and upward. Nevertheless, this is not my *basic* relationship. I am not afraid of the machine. I am not overwhelmed or threatened, because I know I am made in the image of God. I can see why I have mechanical functions and some conditioning, because I have this downward relationship to "lower" things (though, as we shall see, the term "lower" is not ideal). Therefore, intellectually and psychologically, I look at these animals, plants, and machines, and as I face them I understand something of the attitude I should have toward them. I begin to think differently about life. Nature begins to look different. I am separated from it, yet related to it.

Notice the phrase "intellectually and psychologically." This is a very important distinction. I can say, "Yes, the tree is a creature like myself." But that is not all that is involved. There ought to be a psychological insight, too. Psychologically I ought to "feel" a relationship to the tree as my fellow-creature. It is not simply that we ought to feel a relationship intellectually to the tree, and then turn this into just another argument for apologetics, but that we should realize, and train people in our churches to realize, that on the side of creation and on the side of God's infinity and our finiteness we really *are* one with the tree!

This relationship should be not only for aesthetic reasons—though that would be enough reason in itself because beautiful things are important—but we should treat each thing with integrity because it is the way God has made it. So the Christian treats "things" with integrity because we do not believe they are autonomous. Modern man has fallen into a dilemma because he has made things autonomous from God. Simone Weil's statement that modern man lives in a decreated world is acutely perceptive. Everything is decreated; everything is autonomous. But to Christians it is not autonomous, because God made it, and He made things on their own level. The value of the things is not in themselves autonomously, but that God made them—and thus they deserve to be treated with high respect. The tree in the field is to be treated with respect. It is not to be romanticized, as the old lady romanticizes her cat (that is, she reads human reactions into it). This is wrong because it is not true. When you drive the axe into the tree when you need firewood, you are not cutting down a person; you are cutting down a tree. But while we should not romanticize the tree, we must realize God made it and it deserves respect because He made it as a *tree*. Christians who do not believe in the complete evolutionary scale have reason to respect nature as the total evolutionist never can, because we believe God made these things specifically in their own areas. So if we are going to argue against the evolutionists intellectually, we should show the results of our belief in our attitudes. The Christian is a man who has a reason for dealing with each created thing with a high level of respect.

We warned earlier against allowing Platonic concepts to color our Christian thinking. Platonism regards the material as low. But we certainly cannot think the material low when we realize that God created it. We can think of things being created in different orders, but that is a very different concept from thinking things are low in the sense of base, as opposed to high. God made everything, and any sense of lowness (with its poor connotations) has no place here. To think of them as low is really to insult the God who made them.

The second reason why the material is not low is that Christ's body was raised from the dead. This really is a very important point. The resurrection of the body should be held as a doctrinal reality, and further as a truth that gives us an attitude toward life.

Christ's body really was raised from the dead. It could be touched, and He could eat. And this resurrected body is now somewhere. We would reject

Tillich's view of Heaven as a "philosophic other." I think that John Robinson, in *Honest to God*, was right, from his viewpoint, in making the ascension, rather than the resurrection, the crucial point. I think he really understood the implications. A physical resurrection might happen somehow or other in the modern theologian's world, but what you could not have is a body that could eat ascending into "the philosophic other." To the modern theologian, that is an unthinkable concept. In contrast to this, we believe in the ascension; the Bible tells us that the physically resurrected body of Jesus is somewhere in the unseen world.

The resurrection and ascension prove there is no reason to make false dichotomy between the spiritual and the material. That is a totally non-Biblical concept. The material and the spiritual are not opposed. The fact that our bodies are going to be raised also speaks of this.

Another thing to notice from the Biblical viewpoint is God's covenant of creation. God has given us certain written covenants in the Scripture. He has made tremendous promises—for example, the covenant promise to Abraham and to the Jewish people. And He has given the promise to the individual in the New Testament: "He that believeth on the Son hath everlasting life." But with God's written covenants there is also the covenant of creation. The covenant in the Scriptures is a propositional, verbalized covenant; the covenant of creation rests upon the way God made things. God is going to deal with them *as He made them.* God will not violate either covenant. He will always deal with a plant as a plant, with an animal as an animal, with a machine as a machine, and with a man as a man, not violating the orders of creation. He will not ask the machine to behave like a man, neither will He deal with man as though he were a machine.

Thus God treats His creation with integrity: each thing in its own order, each thing the way He made it. If God treats His creation in that way, should we not treat our fellow-creatures with similar integrity? If God treats the tree like a tree, the machine like a machine, the man like a man, shouldn't I, as a fellow-creature, do the same—treating each thing in integrity in its own order? And for the highest reason: because I love God—I love the One who has made it! Loving the Lover who has made it, I have respect for the thing He has made.

Let us emphasize—this is not pantheistic; nevertheless, this respect for all created things must be consciously exercised. *Consciously* we are to treat each thing in its own order and on its own level. Like so many things in the Christian life, this attitude does not come mechanically, because God is treating us like man and expects us to choose and act like man. Thus. we must *consciously* deal with the integrity of each thing that we touch.

The good modern architect struggles to use materials with integrity. Consequently, for example, if he is using poured concrete, he wants it to look like poured concrete and not like brick. Another area of integrity for the architect was emphasized by the great architect Wright, who put forward the concept of the integrity of the building to the integrity of the terrain. So there is this desire in our own day to treat material honestly. If we are to have something beautiful, a landscaping that is going to stand with strength, we shall have to keep in mind the integrity of the terrain and the integrity of the material used. Although this concept is true for all men (since they are made in the image of God, even if they do not know it), yet Christians have a special understanding of it because of their special relationship with God. And our conscious relationship with God is enhanced if we treat all the things He has made in the same way as He treats them.

In sociological things modern man deals only with sociological "averages." But in the modern field of ecology he begins to scream, "I am dying in my city and my ocean is dying." This goes far beyond sociological "averages." His inner attitude to nature is involved. How is he treating it? Modern man has no real "value" for the ocean. All he has is the most crass form of egoist, pragmatic value for it. He treats it as a "thing" in the worst possible sense, to exploit it for the "good" of man. The man who believes things are there only by chance cannot give things a real intrinsic value. But for the Christian, there is an intrinsic value. The value of a thing is not in itself autonomously, but because God made it. It deserves this respect as something which was created by God, as man himself has been created by God.

It is true, as Lynn White points out, that many "Christians" are worse off in the area of ecology than animists, who think there are spirits in the trees and so they don't cut down the trees carelessly. However, although this is true, it is not because Christianity does not have the answer, but because we have not acted on the answer; not because Christianity does not have a view that gives a greater value to the tree than the animist can give it, but because we haven't acted on the value that we know, or should know, it has as a creature of God.

This is an extension of Abraham Kuyper's sphere concept. He saw each of us as many men: the man in the state, the man who is the employer, the man who is the father, the elder in the church, the professor in the university—each of these in a different sphere. But even though they are in different spheres at different times, Christians are to act like Christians *in each of the spheres*. The man is *always* there and he is always a Christian under the norms of Scripture, whether in the classroom or at home.

Now, here is the extension: I am a Christian, but not only a Christian. I am also the creature, the one who has been created; the one who is not autonomous, dealing with these other things that equally are not autonomous. As a Christian, I am consciously to deal with every other created thing with integrity, each thing *in its proper sphere* by creation.

To summarize this chapter, let us reiterate the fundamental fact that God has made all men and all things. He has made my body as well as my soul. He has made me as I am, with the hungers of my spirit and my body. And he has made all things, just as He has made me. He has made the stone, the star, the farthest reaches of the cosmos. He has done all this!

To think of any of these things as intrinsically low is really an insult to the God who made it. Why do Christians lose their way when it seems so clear and so definite? Why should I say my body is lower than my soul when God made both my body and my soul?

Second, Christ's incarnation teaches us that the body of man and nature is not to be considered as low. After all, Jesus took on a real body because God had made man with a body. So, in the incarnation the God of creation took on a human body. More than that, after the resurrection Jesus Christ could eat and be touched. The Bible insists on the real, historic, space-time resurrection of Jesus, so that there was a resurrected body that could eat and that could be touched. This body was not just an apparition or a "ghost." And this same body ascended into Heaven and went into the unseen world. The body that can eat is still in the unseen world, and will one day in future history be visible in the seen world again.

Our resurrection is of the same kind. When Christ comes back again, our bodies are going to be raised from the dead. It is going to be a real physical resurrection, and consequently whether it is Jesus' body or our body the emphasis is the same: God has made the body, and the body is not to be despised and considered as low.

The same sort of emphasis is found explicitly in God's covenant of creation at the time of Noah. In Genesis 9:8-17 we have God's covenant within the relationship to creation. "And I, behold, I establish my covenant with you [mankind], and with your seed after you; and with every living created thing." So God says this, His covenant, was with mankind, but equally with all creation. Then again, in the thirteenth verse, He says: "I do set my bow in the cloud for a token of the covenant between me and the *earth.*" God makes a promise here that embodies *all* creation. God is interested in creation. He does not despise it. There is no reason whatsoever, and it is absolutely false Biblically, for the Christian to have a Platonic view of nature. What God has made, I, who am also a creature, must not despise.

Five

A Substantial Healing

In Romans 8 Paul looks ahead to what is going to happen when Jesus Christ comes back again. He writes: "For the earnest expectation of the creation waiteth for the manifestation of the sons of God [the Christians]. For the creation was made subject to vanity [i. e., frustration], not willingly, but by reason of him who hath subjected the same in hope. Because the creation itself also shall be delivered from the bondage of corruption into the glorious liberty of the children of God. For we know that the whole creation groaneth and travaileth in pain together until now. And not only they, but ourselves also, who have the first fruits of the Spirit [i.e., the Christians], even we ourselves groan within ourselves, waiting for the adoption, that is, the redemption of our body."

What Paul says there is that when our bodies are raised from the dead, at that time nature too will be redeemed. The blood of the Lamb will redeem man and nature together. There is a parallel here to the time of Moses in Egypt when the blood applied to the doorposts saved not only the sons of the Hebrews, but also their animals.

As we stressed in the last chapter, the Bible has no place at all for Platonic distinctions about nature. As Christ's death redeems men, including their bodies, from the consequences of the Fall, so His death will redeem all nature from the Fall's evil consequences at the time when we are raised from the dead.

In Romans 6 Paul applies this future principle to our present situation. It is the great principle of Christian spirituality. Christ died, Christ is our Savior, Christ is coming back again to raise us from the dead. So by faith—because this is true to what has been in Christ's death and to what will be when He comes again, by faith, in the power of the Holy Spirit—we are to live this way substantially now. "Now if we be dead with Christ, we believe that we shall also live with him. Likewise, reckon ye also yourselves to be dead indeed unto sin, but alive unto God through Jesus Christ, our Lord." So we look forward to this, and one day it will be perfect. But we should be looking now, on the basis of the work of Christ, for substantial healing in every area affected by the Fall.

We must understand that even in our relationship with God, a distinction has to be made here. By justification our guilt was completely removed, in a forensic way, as God declared our guilt gone when we accepted Christ as our Savior. But in practice, in our lives between becoming a Christian and the second coming of Christ or our death, we are not in a perfect relationship to God. Therefore, real spirituality lies in the existential, moment-by-moment looking to the work of Christ—seeking and asking God in faith for a substantial reality in our relationship with Him at the present moment. I must be doing this so that substantially, in practice, at this moment, there will be a reality in my relationship with the personal God who is there.

This is also true in other areas, because the Fall, as the Reformation theology has always emphasized, not only separated man from God, but also caused other deep separations. It is interesting that almost the whole "curse" in Genesis 3 is centered upon the outward manifestations. It is the *earth* that is going to be cursed for man's sake. It is the woman's *body* that is involved in the pain of childbirth.

So there are other divisions. Man was divided

from God, first; and then, ever since the Fall, man is separated from himself. These are the psychological divisions. I am convinced that this is the basic psychosis: that the individual man is divided from himself as a result of the Fall.

The next division is that man is divided from other men; these are the sociological divisions. And then man is divided from nature, and nature is divided from nature. So there are these multiple divisions, and one day, when Christ comes back, there is going to be a complete healing of all of them, on the basis of the "blood of the Lamb."

But Christians who believe the Bible are not simply called to say that "one day" there will be healing, but that by God's grace, upon the basis of the work of Christ, substantial healing can be a reality here and now.

Here the church—the orthodox, Bible-believing church—has been really poor. What have we done to heal sociological divisions? Often our churches are a scandal; they are cruel not only to the man "outside," but also to the man "inside."

The same thing is true psychologically. We load people with psychological problems by telling them that "Christians don't have breakdowns," and that is a kind of murder.

On the other hand, what we should have, individually and corporately, is a situation where, on the basis of the work of Christ, Christianity is seen to be not just "pie in the sky," but something that has in it the possibility of substantial healings now in every area where there are divisions because of the Fall. First of all, my division from God is healed by justification, but then there must be the "existential reality" of this moment by moment. Second, there is the psychological division of man from himself. Third, the sociological divisions of man from other men. And last, the division of man from nature, and nature from nature. In all of these areas we should do what we can to bring forth substantial healing.

I took a long while to settle on that word "substantially," but it is, I think, the right word. It conveys the idea of a healing that is not *perfect*, but nevertheless is real and evident. Because of past history and future history, we are called upon to live this way now by faith.

When we carry these ideas over into the area of our relationship to nature, there is an exact parallel. On the basis of the fact that there is going to be total redemption in the future, not only of man but of all creation, the Christian who believes the Bible should be the man who—with God's help and in the power of the Holy Spirit—is treating nature now in the direction of the way nature will be then.

It will not now be perfect, but there should be something substantial or we have missed our calling. God's calling to the Christian now, and to the Christian community, in the area of nature (just as it is in the area of personal Christian living in true spirituality) is that we should exhibit a substantial healing here and now, between man and nature and nature and itself, as far as Christians can bring it to pass.

In *Novum Organum Scientiarum* Francis Bacon wrote: "Man by the fall fell at the same time from his state of innocence and from his dominion over nature. Both of these losses, however, even in this life, can in some part be repaired; the former by religion and faith, the latter by the arts and sciences." It is a tragedy that the church, including the orthodox, evangelical church, has not always remembered that. Here, in this present life, it is possible for the Christian to have some share, through sciences and the arts, in returning nature to its proper place.

But how is this to be achieved? First, as we have seen, by the emphasis upon creation. Then, second, by a fresh understanding of man's "dominion" over nature (Genesis 1:28). Man has dominion over the "lower" orders of creation, but he is not sovereign over them. Only God is the Sovereign Lord, and the lower orders are to be used with this truth in mind. Man is not using his own possessions.

A parallel is the gift of economic possessions. They are to be used as God means them to be used. In the parable of the talents, told by Jesus (Matthew 25:15ff.), the talents or money did not belong to the man with whom they were left. He was a servant and a steward, and he held them only in stewardship for the true Owner.

It is the same when we have dominion over nature: *it is not ours*. It belongs to God, and we are to exercise our dominion over these things not as though entitled to exploit them, but as things borrowed or held in trust. We are to use them realizing that they are not ours intrinsically. Man's dominion is under God's dominion.

Whenever anything is made autonomous, as I stressed in *Escape from Reason*, nature "eats up" grace, and soon all meaning is gone. And that is true here. When nature is made autonomous, either by the materialist or by the Christian when he slips over and sits in the wrong place, soon *man eats up nature*. That is what we are seeing today. Suddenly man is beginning to scream, and I am convinced God is permitting these things to come to pass. The problem is not the growth of population alone, nor technical growth alone—those could be handled.

The problem, as White correctly points out, is the philosophy with which man has looked on nature.

An essential part of a true philosophy is a correct understanding of the pattern and plan of creation as revealed by the God who made it. For instance, we must see that each step "higher"—the machine, the plant, the animal, and man—has the use of that which is lower than itself. We find that man calls upon and utilizes the animal, the plant, and the machine; the animal eats the plant. The plant utilizes the machine portion of the universe. Each thing in God's creation utilizes the thing that God has made under it.

We must also appreciate that each thing is limited by what it is. That is, a plant is limited by being a plant, but it is also limited by the properties of those things under it that it uses. So the plant can only use the chemicals on the basis of the boundary condition of the chemicals' properties. There is nothing else it can do.

But this is true also for man. We cannot make our own universe; we can only use what is under us in the order of creation. But there is a difference, and that is that the animal, for example, must use the lower *as what it is*. Man has to accept some necessary limitations of what is under him, but he can *consciously* act upon what is there. That is a real difference. The animal simply eats the plant. He cannot change its situation or properties. The man, on the other hand, has to accept limitations, but nevertheless is called upon in his relationship to nature to treat the thing that is under him *consciously*, on the basis of what God has made it to be. The animal, the plant *must* do it; the man *should* do it. We are to use it, but we are not to use it as though it were nothing in itself

Now let us look at it in another way. Man was given dominion over creation. This is true. But since the Fall man has exercised this dominion wrongly. He is a rebel who has set himself at the center of the universe. By creation man has dominion, but as a fallen creature he has used that dominion wrongly. Because he is fallen, he exploits created things as though they were nothing in themselves, and as though he has an autonomous right to them.

Surely then, Christians who have returned, through the work of the Lord Jesus Christ, to fellowship with God and have a proper place of reference to the God who is there should demonstrate a proper use of nature. We are to have dominion over it, but we are not going to use it as fallen man uses it. We are not going to act as though it were nothing in itself or as though we will do to nature everything we can do.

A parallel is man's dominion over woman. At the Fall man was given dominion in the home over the woman. But fallen man takes this and turns it into tyranny and makes his wife a slave. So first in the Judaic teaching—the Old Testament law—and then later and more specifically in the New Testament, man is taught to exercise dominion without tyranny. The man is to be the head of the home, but the man is also to love his wife as Christ loves the church. Thus everything is back in its right place. There is to be order in the midst of a fallen world, but in love.

So fallen man has dominion over nature, but he uses it wrongly. The Christian is called upon to exhibit this dominion, but to exhibit it rightly: treating the thing as having value in itself, exercising dominion without being destructive. The church should always have taught and done this, but it has generally failed to do so, and we need to confess our failure. Francis Bacon understood this, and so have other Christians at different times; but by and large we must say that for a long, long time Christian teachers, including the best orthodox theologians, have shown a real poverty here.

As a parallel example, what would have happened if the church at the time of the Industrial Revolution had spoken out against the economic abuses which arose from it? This is not to suggest that the Industrial Revolution was wrong, or that private property as such is wrong, but that the church at a point in history when it had the consensus failed (with some notable exceptions) to speak against the abuse of economic dominion. So also the church has not spoken out as it should have done throughout history against the abuse of nature.

But when the church puts belief into practice, in relationship to man *and to nature*, there is substantial healing. One of the first fruits of that healing is a new sense of beauty. The aesthetic values are not to be despised. God has made man with a sense of beauty no animal has; no animal has ever produced a work of art. Man as made in the image of God has an aesthetic quality, and as soon as he begins to deal with nature as he should, beauty is preserved in nature. But also, economic and human value accrue, for the problems of ecology that we have now will diminish.

Christians should be able to exhibit individually and corporately that on the basis of the work of Christ, dealing with things according to the worldview and basic philosophy of the Bible, they can produce something that the world has tried, but failed, to produce. The Christian community should be a living exhibition of the truth that in our present situation it is possible to have substantial sociological healings—healings that humanism longs for, but has not been able to produce. Humanism is not wrong in its cry for sociological healing, but humanism is not producing it. And the same thing is true in regard to a substantial healing where nature is concerned.

So we find that when we begin to deal on a Christian basis, things begin to change—not just in theory but in practice. Man is not to be sacrificed, as pantheism sacrifices him, because after all he was made in the image of God and given dominion. And yet nature is to be honored, each thing on its own level. In other words, there is a balance here. Man has dominion; he has a right by choice, because he is a moral creature, a right by choice to have dominion. But he is also by choice to exercise it rightly. He is to honor what God has made, up to the very highest level that he can honor it, without sacrificing man.

Christians, of all people, should not be the destroyers. We should treat nature with an overwhelming respect. We may cut down a tree to build a house, or to make a fire to keep the family warm. But we should not cut down the tree just to cut down the tree. We may, if necessary, bark the cork tree in order to have the use of the bark. But what we should not do is to bark the tree simply for the sake of doing so, and let it dry and stand there a dead skeleton in the wind. To do so is not to treat the tree with integrity. We have the right to rid our houses of ants; but what we have not the right to do is to forget to honor the ant as God made it, in its rightful place in nature. When we meet the ant on the sidewalk, we step over him. He is a creature, like ourselves; not made in the image of God, but equal with man as far as creation is concerned. The ant and the man are both creatures.

In this sense Saint Francis's use of the term "brothers to the birds" is not only theologically correct, but a thing to be intellectually thought of and practically practiced. More, it is to be psychologically felt as I face the tree, the bird, the ant. If this was what the The Doors meant when they spoke of "our fair sister," it would have been beautiful. Used correctly in the Christian framework, that expression is magnificent. Why have orthodox, evangelical Christians produced few hymns putting such a beautiful concept in a proper theological setting?

One does not deface things simply to deface them. After all, the rock has a God-given right to be a rock as He made it. If you must move the rock in order to build the foundation of a house, then by all means move it. But on a walk in the woods do not strip the moss from it for no reason, and then leave the moss to lie by the side and die. Even the moss has a right to live. It is equal with man as a creature of God.

Hunting game is another example of the same principle. Killing animals for food is one thing, but on the other hand they do not exist simply as things to be slaughtered. This is true of fishing, too. Many men fish and leave their victims to rot and stink. But what about the fish? Has it no rights—not to be romanticized as though he were a man—but real rights? On the one hand, it is wrong to treat the fish as though it were a human baby; on the other hand, neither is it a chip of wood or a stone.

When we consider the tree, which is "below" the fish, we may chop it down, so long as we remember it is a tree, with its own value *as a tree*. It is not a zero. Some of our housing developments demonstrate the practical application of this. Bulldozers have gone in to flatten everything and clear the trees before the houses are begun. The end result is ugliness. It would have cost another thousand dollars to bulldoze *around* the trees, so they are simply bulldozed down without question. And then we wonder, looking at the result, how people can live there. It is less human in its barrenness, and even economically it is poorer as the topsoil washes away. So when man breaks God's truth, in reality he suffers.

The hippies of the 1960s were right in their desire to be close to nature, even walking in bare feet in order to feel it. But they had no sufficient philosophy, and so their views drifted into pantheism and soon became ugly. But Christians, who should understand the creation principle, have a reason for respecting nature, and when they do, it results in benefits to man. Let us be clear: this is not just a pragmatic attitude; there is a basis for it. We treat nature with respect because God made it. When an orthodox, evangelical Christian mistreats or is insensible to nature, *at that point* he is more wrong than the hippie who had no real basis for his feeling for nature and yet sensed that man and nature should have a relationship beyond that of spoiler and spoiled. You may or may not want to walk barefoot to feel close to nature, but as a *Christian* what relationship have you thought of and practiced toward nature as your fellow-creature?

Why do I have an emotional reaction toward the tree? For some abstract or pragmatic reason? Not at all. Secular man may say he cares for the tree because if he cuts it down, his cities will not be able to breathe. But that is egoism, and egoism will produce ugliness, no matter how long it takes or what fine words are used. On this basis technology will continue to take another twist on the garrote of both nature and man. But the Christian stands in front of the tree and has an emotional reaction toward it, because the tree has a real value in itself being a creature made by God. I have this in common with the tree: we were made by God and not just cast up by chance.

Suddenly then we have real beauty. Life begins to breathe. For us the world begins to breathe as it never breathed before. We can love a man for his own sake, for we know who the man is—he is made in the image of God. And we can care for the animal, the tree, and even the machine portion of the universe, each thing in its own order—for we know it to be a fellow-creature with ourselves, both made by the same God.

Six

The Christian View: The "Pilot Plant"

So we have seen that a truly Biblical Christianity has a real answer to the ecological crisis. It offers a balanced and healthy attitude to nature, arising from the truth of its creation by God. It offers the hope here and now of substantial healing in nature of some of the results of the Fall, arising from the truth of redemption in Christ. In each of the alienations arising from the Fall, Christians, individually and corporately, should consciously in practice be a healing redemptive factor—in the separation of man from God, of man from himself, of man from man, of man from nature, and of nature from nature.

A Christian-based science and technology should consciously try to see nature substantially healed, while waiting for the future complete healing at Christ's return. In this chapter, we must ask how the Christian church, believing these truths, can apply them practically to the question of ecology.

For here is our calling. We must exhibit that on the basis of the work of Christ the church can achieve partially, but substantially, what the secular world wants and cannot get. The church ought to be a "pilot plant," where men can see in our congregations and missions a substantial healing of all the divisions, the alienations which man's rebellion has produced.

Let me explain that phrase "pilot plant." When an industrial company is about to construct a big factory, they first of all make a pilot plant. This is to demonstrate that the full-scale plant will work. Now the church, I believe, ought to be a pilot plant in regard to the healing of man and himself, of man and man, and man and nature. Indeed, unless something like this happens, I do not believe the world will listen to what we have to say. For instance, in the area of nature, we ought to be exhibiting the very opposite of the situation I described earlier, where the pagans who had their wine stomps provided a beautiful setting for the Christians to look at, while the Christians provided something ugly for the pagans to see. That sort of situation should be reversed, or our words and our philosophy will, predictably, be ignored.

So the Christian church ought to be this "pilot plant," through individual attitudes and the Christian community's attitude, to exhibit that in this present life man can exercise dominion over nature without being destructive. Let me give two illustrations of what this might involve. The first is open-face or strip mining.

Why has strip mining usually turned the area where it has been used into desert? Why is the "Black Country" in England's Midlands black? What has brought about the ugly destruction of the environment? There is one reason: man's greed.

If the strip miners would take bulldozers and push back the topsoil, rip out the coal, then replace the topsoil, in ten years after the coal was removed there would be a green field, and in fifty years a forest. But as it has usually been practiced, for an added profit above what is reasonable in regard to nature, man turns these areas into deserts and then cries out that the topsoil is gone, grass will not grow, and there is no way to grow trees for hundreds of years!

It is always true that if you treat the land properly, you have to make two choices. The first is in the area of economics. It costs more money, at least at first, to treat the land well. For instance, in the case of the school I have mentioned, all they had to do to improve the place was to plant trees to shield the building they built. But it costs money to plant trees, and somebody decided that instead of planting trees they would prefer to do something else with the money. Of course, the school needs money for its important work; but there is a time when planting trees is an important work.

The second choice involved is that it usually takes longer to treat the land properly. These are the two factors that lead to the destruction of our environment: money and time—or to say it another way, greed and haste. The question is, or seems to be, are we going to have an immediate profit and an immediate saving of time, or are we going to do what we really should do as God's children?

Apply this to strip mining. There is no reason why strip mining had to leave western Pennsylvania or eastern Kentucky in its present condition. Strip mines, as we have seen, do not have to be left this way; the top soil can be bulldozed back. What we, the Christian community, have to do is to refuse men the right to ravish our land, just as we refuse them the right to ravish our women; to insist that somebody accept a little less profit by not exploiting nature. And the first step is exhibiting the fact that as individual Christians and as Christian communities we ourselves do not ravish our fair sister for the sake of greed in one form or another.

We can see the same sort of thing happening in Switzerland. Here is a village up in the mountains. It has never had electricity. The people have managed well for a thousand years without electricity. Now suddenly "civilization" comes, and everybody knows that you cannot have "civilization" without electricity, so the decision is made to give the village electrical power.

This can be done in one of two ways. They can have their electricity in about three months: just chop off everything, tear the forest in pieces, run big, heavy wires over the whole thing, and create ugliness out of what was beautiful. Or they can wait a couple of years for their electricity; they can handle the cables and the forests with more care, hiding what they need to hide and considering the integrity of the environment, and end up with something infinitely preferable. They have their electricity and the village has its beauty, and the only cost is to add two years to the thousand years that they have been without electricity. There would be some economic factors here, but the largest one is that of sheer haste.

Happily, in Switzerland in the last few years in certain places more things are being done in this direction. For example, in our village all the telephone wires have been put under the ground. This has made a very different impression: one now sees an uncluttered village in the Alps. This is so, even if the person now arriving at the village for the first time did not know the contrast to what it was previously.

One can also think of the highways—the asphalt jungle in the United States. Think, if you will, of the way the bulldozers are often used across the Swiss mountains. *Almost always* the scars and the ugliness are the results of hurry. And whether it is hurry or greed, these things eat away at nature.

What can be done was shown in the highway built near Castle Chillon in Switzerland. Both care and money were taken in building a bridgelike construction, high, behind and away from the castle, and the beauty of the site was not destroyed.

As Christians we have to learn to say "Stop!" because after all, greed is destructive of nature at this point, and there is a time to take one's time.

Now all this does not come about automatically. Science today treats man as less than man, and nature as less than nature. And the reason for this is that modern science has the wrong sense of *origin*; and having the wrong sense of origin, it has no category sufficient to treat nature as nature any more than it has to treat man as man.

Nevertheless, we who are Christians must be careful. We must confess that we missed our opportunity. We have spoken loudly against materialistic science, but we have done little to show that in practice we ourselves as Christians are not dominated by a technological orientation in regard either to man or nature. We should have been stressing and practicing for a long time that there is a basic reason why we should not do all that with our technology we can do. We have missed the opportunity to help man save his earth. Not only that, but in our generation we are losing an evangelistic opportunity because when modern people have a real sensitivity to nature, many of them turn to the pantheistic mentality. They have seen that most Christians simply do not care about nature as such.

So we have not only missed our opportunity to save the earth for man, but this also partly accounts for the fact that we have largely missed the opportunity of reaching the twentieth century. These are reasons why the church seems irrelevant and helpless in our generation. We are living in and practicing a sub-Christianity.

There is a parallel between man's misuse of

nature and man's misuse of man. We can this in two areas.

First of all, let us think of the sex relationship. What is man's attitude towards the girl? It is possible, and common in the modern setting, to have a "playboy" attitude, or rather a "plaything" attitude, where the "playmate" becomes the "plaything." Here, the girl is no more than a sex object.

But what is the Christian view? Somebody may offer at this point the rather romantic notion, "You shouldn't look for any pleasure for yourself; you should just look for the other person's pleasure." But that is not what the Bible says. We are to love our neighbor as *ourselves*. We have a right to pleasure, too. But what we do not have a right to do is to forget that the girl is a person and not an animal, or a plant, or a machine. We have the right to have our pleasure in a sexual relationship, but we have no right whatsoever to exploit a partner as a sex object.

There should be a conscious limitation upon our pleasure. We impose a limit—a *self-imposed limit*—in order to treat the wife fairly as a person. So although a husband could do more, he does not do everything he could do, because he must treat her also as a person and not just as a thing with no value. And if he does so treat her, eventually he loses, because love is gone, and all that is left is just a mechanical, chemical sexuality; humanity is lost as he treats her as less than human. Eventually not only her humanity is diminished, but his as well. In contrast, if he does less than he could do, eventually he has more, for he has a human relationship; he has love and not just a physical act. It is like the principle of the boomerang—it can come full circle and destroy the destroyer. *And that is exactly what happens with nature.* If we treat nature as having no intrinsic value, our own value is diminished.

A second parallel may be found with man in business. We have all kinds of idealists today who cry, "No profit! Down with the profit motive!" But men do not work this way. Even communism is learning the need to reinstate the profit motive. And certainly the Bible does not say that the profit motive is wrong.

But I am to treat the man I deal with in business *as myself.* I am to "love" him as my neighbor, and as myself. It is perfectly right that I should have some profit, but I must not get it by treating him (or exploiting him) as a consumer object. If I do this, eventually I shall destroy not him alone, but myself as well, because I shall have lowered the real value of myself.

So, just as the girl is not to be treated as a sex object but as a person, so again I must, if I am a businessman functioning on a Christian basis, realize I am dealing with another man made in the image of God, and I must impose some conscious limitation on myself. The Christian businessman will take profit, but he will not do everything he could do in exacting all the profit he could exact.

The Old Testament is very plain at this point: "If you take a man's cloak for a collateral, be sure to give it back to him every night, because he might be cold at night" (Exodus 22:26). Again: "No man shall take a man's life to pledge" (Deuteronomy 24:6). That shows a very different mentality from that which often marks Christian businessmen. It may be properly called the right of private property, but it is a very different kind of right of private property. It realizes that if we treat other men in business or in industry as machines, we make ourselves machines, because we are not more than they are. Indeed, if we make other men and ourselves machines in commercial relationships, gradually this will penetrate every area of life and the wonder of humanity will begin to disappear.

Thus again, the Christian does not do all he can do. He has a limiting principle; and in doing less, he has more, for his own humanness is at stake. A girl should not be treated as a sex object to be used simply for pleasure. A man should not be treated as a consumer object simply for bigger profit. In the area of sex, and in the area of business, to treat persons as they should be treated, on the basis of the creation of God, is not only right in itself but produces good results, because our own humanity begins to bloom.

In the area of nature it is exactly the same. If nature is only a meaningless particular, is "decreated," to use Simone Weil's evocative word, with no universal to give it meaning, then the wonder is gone from it. Unless there is a universal over the particulars, there is no meaning.

Jean-Paul Sartre picked this up: "If you have a finite point and it has no infinite reference point, then that finite point is absurd." He was right, and unhappily that is where he himself was—an absurd particular in the midst of only absurd particulars.

So if nature and the things of nature are only a meaningless series of particulars in a decreated universe, with no universal to give them meaning, then nature is become absurd, the wonder is gone from it. And wonder is equally gone from me, because I too am a finite thing.

But Christians insist that we do have a universal. God is there! The personal-infinite God is the universal of all the particulars, because He created all the particulars; and in His verbalized, propositional communications in the Scripture He has given us categories within which to treat everything within His creation: man to man, man to nature, the whole lot.

Now both the thing that He has made and I, who am also made by Him, have wonder, awe, and real value. But we must remember that the value I consciously put on a thing will finally be my own value, for I too am finite. If I let the wonder go from the thing, soon the wonder will go from mankind and me. And this is where people live today. The wonder is all gone. Man sits in his autonomous, "decreated" world, where there are no universals and no wonder in nature. Indeed, in an arrogant and egoistic way, nature has been reduced to a "thing" for man to use or exploit.

And if modern man speaks of protecting the ecological balance of nature, it is only on the pragmatic level for man, with no basis for nature's having any real value in itself. And thus man too is reduced another notch in value, and dehumanized technology takes another turn on the vise.

On the other hand, in the Christian view of things nature is restored. Suddenly the wonder returns.

But it is not enough merely as a matter of theory to believe that there is a real meaning in nature.

The truth has to be practiced consciously. We have to begin to treat nature the way it *should* be treated.

We have seen in regard to the pleasure of sex, and in the making of profit in industry and business, that man must voluntarily limit himself. He must not be driven either for greed or haste to remove all the self-limitations. Or we can put it in another way: we must not allow ourselves individually, nor our technology, to do everything we or it can do.

The animal can make no conscious limitation. The cow eats the grass—it has no decision to make; it cannot do otherwise. Its only limitation is the mechanical limitation of its "cowness." I who am made in the image of God can make a choice. I am able to do things to nature that I should not do. So I am to put a *self*-limitation on what is possible. The horror and ugliness of modern man in his technology and in his individual life is that he does everything he can do, without limitation. Everything he *can* do, he *does*. He kills the world, he kills mankind, and he kills himself.

I am a being made in the image of God. Having a rational-moral limitation, not everything man can do is right to do. Indeed, this is the problem all the way back to the Garden of Eden. From the point of view of body structure, Eve could eat the fruit; Adam could eat the fruit. But on the basis of the second boundary condition of the moral command of God, and the character of God, it was wrong for them to eat the fruit. The call was for Eve to limit herself: to refrain from doing something she could do.

Technologically, modern man does everything he can do; he functions on this single boundary principle. Modern man, seeing himself as autonomous, with no personal-infinite God who has spoken, has no adequate universal to supply an adequate second boundary condition; and man, being fallen, is not only finite, but sinful. Thus man's pragmatic choices have no reference point beyond human egotism. It is dog eat dog, man eat man, man eat nature. Man with his greed has no real reason not to rape nature and treat it as a reverse "consumer object." He sees nature as without value or rights.

In conclusion, then, we may say that if things are treated only as autonomous machines in a decreated world, they are finally meaningless. But if that is so, then inevitably so am I—man—equally autonomous and also equally meaningless. But if individually and in the Christian community I treat the things which God has made with integrity and treat them this way lovingly, because they are His, things change.

If I love the Lover, I love what the Lover has made. Perhaps this is the reason why so many Christians feel an unreality in their Christian lives. If I don't love what the Lover has made—in the area of man, in the area of nature—and really love it because He made it, do I really love the Lover?

It is easy to make professions of faith, but they may not be worth much because they have little meaning. They may become merely a mental assent that means little or nothing.

But I must be clear that I am not loving the tree or whatever is standing in front of me for a pragmatic reason. It will have a pragmatic *result*, the very pragmatic results that the men involved in ecology are looking for. But as a Christian I do not do it for the practical or pragmatic results; I do it because it is right and because God is the Maker. And then suddenly things drop into place.

There are things before me which I now face, not as a cow would face the buttercup—merely the mechanical situation—but facing it by choice. I look at the buttercup, and I treat the buttercup the way it should be treated. The buttercup and I are both created by God; but beyond this, I can treat it properly by personal choice. I act personally, and I am a person! Psychologically I begin to breathe and live. Psychologically I am now dealing on a personal level, not only with men and women, but also with the things in nature that God has made which are less than personal in themselves, and the old hang-ups begin to crumble. My humanness grows, and the modern technological pit and pendulum is no longer closing in on me.

As a result, then, there is beauty instead of a desert. The question of aesthetics is also in place. This surely is something that has importance in itself and is not to be despised. Beauty does not have to have pragmatic reasons to have value. So if we did nothing else in our Christian view of nature than to save and enjoy beauty, it would be of value and worthwhile.

But it is not only that, as we have seen. The balance of nature will be more nearly what it should be, and there will be a way to utilize nature for man and yet not destroy the resources which man needs. But none of this will happen if it is only a gimmick. We have to be in the right relationship with Him in the way He has provided, and then, as Christians, have and practice the Christian view of nature.

When we have learned this—the Christian view of nature—then there can be a real ecology; beauty will flow, psychological freedom will come, and the world will cease to be turned into a desert. Because it is right, on the basis of the whole

Christian system—which is strong enough to stand it all because it is true—as I face the buttercup, I say: "Fellow-creature, fellow-*creature*, I won't walk on you. We are both creatures together."

Concluding Chapter

by
Udo Middelmann

When Francis Schaeffer wrote *Pollution and the Death of Man* in 1970, this short book addressed a surprisingly large number of "environmental" issues which were just beginning to break into the public discourse. As those issues began to be raised, our way of life would be questioned and various remedial actions would be demanded in public and in private. No day would pass without new and alarming details of human carelessness and irresponsible, sometimes even criminal actions.

We became aware that our survival as human beings could no longer be guaranteed. Death not in a foreign war but by our own action seemed more likely in a world of landfills, off-shore spills, toxic wastes, population explosion, and ozone depletion.

Insufficiency and efforts to conserve scarce resources are not new phenomena. Our ancestors had often fled from homelands plagued by poverty, political persecution, or poor resources. Even our parents and some of us remember recycling old metal, glass—even rags and bones. My earliest pocket money came from scavenging through ruins after the Second World War in Europe.

Yet when the warning bell was rung, calling us to save our endangered earth, memories of such responsible efforts in the past had faded. Technology was giving us more and more consumer goods at ever lower prices, and collecting, sorting, and reuse seemed itself primitive and unnecessary. The wider use of the automobile had created visual and physical distance from things thrown away. Household and industrial waste were discarded far from the places where they had been produced and consumed. "Out of sight, out of mind" made sense in a world at peace with itself.

The Western world was demonstrating its superiority through progress available to all at reduced cost. Stalin's children had promised that their system would outperform ours in a matter of some twenty-five years; but we were well on our way to showing *them* that a people with material abundance would not only be better off, but would also be a light in a world of darkness.

We must put ourselves back into the hopes and feelings of that time in order to understand more fully the changes in attitude that have taken place since then. As our world has shrunk, through better transportation and communication, we have become far more aware of the threats to all of life. We are more aware that our living space, the air we breathe, and the water we drink are polluted—more so than we could have imagined during those days of unlimited growth.

My children are once again recycling; they know the value of discarded objects. They respond positively to calls for environmental responsibility. They have access to an abundance of books, television programs, and films with ecological themes. They understand that they must show restraint in consuming the resources their own children will need.

They are also more pessimistic than my generation about the future of our planet. They are more sensitive, but also more afraid and filled with guilt. They have been made to be doubtful and angry about our Western outlook on mankind and his environment. They talk more often about a spoiled and mistreated earth. They can easily identify "eco-sinners." To their generation, the color green spells peace and survival. *Bio*, used as a prefix, stimulates their moral sense. Their information comes from school, from field trips, and "sensitizing" experiences. Of course they still use automobiles to go on those trips. They toss away their garbage with little remorse. Yet they are, undeniably, more aware of environmental concerns than were Schaeffer's first readers.

Schaeffer wrote before the oil shock of 1973. He wrote in response to a nascent criticism of Christianity as the source of environmental problems. His concern was not only that a neglect of the environment would spell the death of man by a destruction of our life-support system. He was also concerned that the death of man might be brought about by the very environmental programs claiming to seek his salvation.

This greater danger has not been adequately understood. The urgency of the immediate perils addressed by many environmentalist groups have often obscured the fact that the loudest advocates of change have also wanted to change our view of the human being, and of life itself, away from the Biblical basis of our culture and our moral concerns.

These environmentalists did not limit their agenda to attack immoral acts by irresponsible people, institutions, and corporations. They went to the root of what we know as Western civilization—the value of each person under God, even in a fallen world characterized by a broken nature. Not only the *acts* of man should change, said these environmentalists: man's understanding of himself should be radically redirected to a more Eastern view, where man merges with everything.

While Schaeffer addressed the physical problems of a polluted earth, he also dealt with the environmentalists' challenges to the Bible's teaching about man and nature. He showed that the Bible, while elevating man to have dominion, also calls him to self-examination and repentance—including repentance of his "environmental sins." But repentance, he showed, should never lead to the abolition of the sinner. Rather, it should lead to his restoration and redirection as an individual actor in the art of life.

The Bible emphasizes individual choice and significance. Man is the crown of creation. Males and females are stewards responsible to God, not to nature. But in fulfilling that responsibility, they seek ways to improve and safeguard their earthly environment. Western culture, with its high view of individual responsibility, its drive to advance itself technologically and democratically, has its roots in the Bible.

Yet this affirmation of the significance of each individual person, rooted in the Bible and so central to the rise of Western civilization, is now blamed for all the evils of society—even though without it none of the problems would have been noticed and fought against in the first place. It is always the sensitive person who stands out of the crowd and warns against evil. For the environmentalist to deny the Biblical notion of individual worth, and to prefer the Eastern view of man, is to saw off the branch on which he sits.

The timing of the current environmental debate is interesting. Earlier warnings in this century about dangers to the environment have been heeded, and remedies often found. The history of science, including social science, is also the history of human efforts to diminish disaster. But the current debate is taking place in a time of increasing doubt about our culture's ability to work toward solutions. The 1969 oil blow-out in the Santa Barbara Channel, the fire on the Cuyahoga River in Cleveland, and similar events were seen as evidence of technology and rationality having taken the place of spiritual values—evidence of a lack of moral concern in a world reduced to the pursuit of profit and technological advancement.

In reaction, the drug culture had advocated Eastern spiritual values. The Beatles and Timothy Leary had told us about the need to run from a culture of concrete, metal, oil, and pollution, to Eastern values. "Flower power" would provide for a humane dimension in a world of materialism.

External events in rapid succession fueled a fear of imminent hazard and death, in a society pampered in safety and high expectations and yet beginning to doubt its place in the global village. Biblical convictions had weakened. A shallow view of the history and geography of ideas—without a vital understanding of historic Christianity—was fostered by an increasingly more privatized faith of personal experience. The courage to struggle and to engage oneself for life was canceled by a fear of creating more problems by such a struggle. The door was opened to a fundamentally different perception of the place of man, the role of nature, and the place and value of individual life.

Industrial power alone could not win the war in Vietnam. Berkeley, Kent State, and Columbia joined Watts and the assassinations of JFK and Martin Luther King, Jr. to demand a different salvation than Christianity—even though its teachings had for centuries brought freedom, significance, and the rule of law to mankind.

The industrialization in the eighteenth and nineteenth centuries had provoked the search for the "noble savage." That search did not succeed, but now, a hundred years later, its ghost has appeared in a new garment. That ghost judges Western views as inferior because Western man repels fate and nature to give shape to human life. According to the Biblical traditional view, man is the steward of God, not of nature. He takes his orders from the Bible, not from the wind or the mountains. This sets him up as an occasional interferer, one who changes the "natural" order into "culture." He looks for iron under every hill and copper under every mountain. He fights disease, poverty, and oblivion for individuals.

But now a new nobility is sought for man, one which harmonizes with the larger whole. God is replaced by the cycles of the year, by the dynamics of an eco-system. Man is to harmonize with the rest of nature. The individual is sacrificed for the well-being of a future anonymous humanity.

There were some good reasons to take stock of and to rethink our Western attitudes on environmental issues. And there have been many beneficial results to the work of the present-day nature lobby.

Products are judged not only for their appearance and power to stimulate sales and provide jobs, but also for their effect on the environment. Legislation has functioned to control damage, set standards, and sensitize the public. Court enforcements, news reports, and public scandals have contributed to more responsible attitudes and practices.

Yet environmentalism has also produced a new set of problems. Competing in the world market has become more difficult, as many of our international competitors do not share our high ecological standards. There has been a moral victory of sorts, but a punitive effect for workers. Jobs have been exported to people who care less about the air they breathe.

This in turn has increased resentment of Western ideas. At the UN, poorer countries have demanded exemption from high environmental standards, or financial aid to comply with those standards, when their own worldview and nationalistic fervor were often the greatest hindrance to development and a concern for their citizens.

Once we put aside the myth of the equality of all cultures and religions, the darkness and frequent inhumanities of non-Christian worldviews become clear. An older form of pollution, resulting from disregard for human life and a resignation to natural suffering, surfaces in many native and non-Christian cultures. It is true that these cultures are sometimes victimized by the imported poison of Western technology; it is equally true that they often take in that poison willingly, for the sake of their own economic advancement and with little concern for its effect on individual human life.

Western, more developed societies need to do more to prevent the export of environmental hazards to lesser developed societies. But that restraint must go hand in hand with a reexamination of worldviews whose traditions have not lamented the loss of life, but rather have accepted it as normal—as merely one more spin of the wheel of fate.

Meanwhile, within our own cultural context the ultimate basis for action, ethics, and law also needs to be addressed. For the lack of a convincing universal morality undermines any effort to bring about a better world through more moral actions.

The immediate stimulus for *Pollution and the Death of Man* was Lynn White's article "The Historical Roots of our Ecological Crisis," in *Science* magazine, which is reprinted in Appendix A. White—like numerous subsequent writers—sees the Christian worldview as the root of present ecological problems. Man has destroyed the environment, says White, because of the Bible's call for man to have dominion over nature. Biblical thinking, more than the sinfulness of the individual, is the culprit, for it calls for an assertive mind-set which does not derive its instruction from nature, but from God. White fails to see how affirmative human actions, mandated by the Creator, can reshape a fallen nature. To him all such efforts are opposed to the harmony of the natural order.

Schaeffer called for repentance of our misuse of nature. But rather than identifying repentance with submission to the dictates of nature or of the community, he defines it as a willful acknowledgment of God's truth and ways. Where modern man served but himself in his rationalistic independence, he is now called not to serve nature in its harmonious "survival of the fittest" patterns, but to return to the recognition that he is a creature before the Creator. We are God's children, not nature's.

Such an understanding will result in a greater concern about nature than will the programs of the materialist or the naturalist. They start with an ultimately impersonal orientation, in which man has no place, no calling. They both demand the sacrifice of human life. The naturalist sacrifices man to nature and abolishes the moral and intellectual life which alone is concerned about justice and the good life. The materialist commits suicide in the selfish, hedonistic pursuit of short-term profit. He denies any responsibility above his ability to succeed. Both pursue their goals without meaning and without reflection. Both crush human life in the end.

Schaeffer wrote *Pollution and the Death of Man* not only from the perspective of the Bible, but also in the context of constant prayer and reflection. He was a vastly experienced person with deep feelings and emotions. After moving to Europe from the United States in 1948, he would never again own a car, relying instead on public transport. His rest and exercise came from hiking in the mountains, following old maps and Roman trails. That contact with nature, and his work in his gardens, was added to his study of the city and of human activities over centuries and to his many trips across the world. History exhibited the world of ideas more than a conquest of land.

Schaeffer crossed the ocean by boat and objected to waste thrown overboard. During his hikes in the mountains, where Romans and Hannibal, traders and traitors, men and maidens, lovers and outlaws had hiked, he would, in the midst of the deepest philosophical discussion with students, bend to pick up a piece of trash and carry it in his knapsack to the next trash bin. He was no mere theological theoretician.

Nor was he a fanatical naturalist who objected to all modern achievements. He was forever against any survival program for nature or for an impersonal future "humanity" when that program denied the value and needs of real individuals living today.

The perspective Schaeffer gained from his study of the Bible and of history was added to by his work with people. He was intensely sensitive to the reality of having to live in a fallen world. For him, only the Biblical account of the space-time fall of man was an adequate explanation for human suffering. And as neighbor to human beings from all backgrounds, there were for him "no little people"—since the God of the Bible had made them and called them individually. While some felt weak and bruised, Schaeffer's effort was to strengthen them in their conviction as Christians, giving sound and coherent answers from the Bible for their most troublesome questions and doubts. He protected each person as if he or she were a temporarily bruised flower.

For Schaeffer the ecological question could not be separated from his larger concerns about man's foolish drive toward either autonomy or oblivion. For without the Bible, there is no knowledge of man's Creator nor of his meaning in this life. With sadness Schaeffer would relate Darwin's admission, in his diary, that he had lost all enjoyment of nature after having proposed the theory of natural selection. There is a purpose in each particle created by God, but the particle itself does not reveal that purpose.

Frequently we are advised to consider other life-models and cultural traditions in order to escape the problems of our own culture. Schaeffer found no solace in these alternatives. To seek a state of closer identification with *anything but the God of the Bible* is fraught with sad results. Man is not to be wrapped into a larger eco-system. That would only prevent him from making those critical judgments about the world and himself which life in a moral universe requires of each of us.

Neither the model of the North American Indians, nor East Indian religions, nor Aboriginal views, nor Asian submission to a "way" present viable alternatives. In the actual teachings of Eastern religions and in the practices of cultures bound to their outlook about man in the cosmos, human beings have not fared well. Their mortality rates are unacceptable. Their mastery of life is often sadly insufficient. They have not produced a more balanced ecology. Where industrial pollution has not been excessive, human and social pollution from lack of sanitation, short life spans, and arbitrary legal rights have created an unacceptable and unnecessary mountain of human suffering.

Anyone who exposes himself to cultures untouched by Christian values finds out quickly that neither the human being nor nature are treated with any great sympathy. Nature suffers together with man quite unnecessarily. Whether it be the cows of India, the wildlife of Africa, the deforested mountains of Nepal, the expanding desert of sub-Saharan Africa, or the land, animals, and people in flood-prone Bangladesh, the problems are not easily labeled as either natural and therefore to be accepted, or Western and therefore to be rejected as the interference of a hostile culture. The Biblical answer that we live in a fallen world without easy solutions is the most sympathetic and concerned answer—and the only one which motivates people to resist an abnormal nature.

The myth of the noble savage has been uncovered. Man everywhere is a sinner; and he loses the contest for life whenever he suppresses the high calling to be a creature made in God's image and sees himself rather as made in the image of nature, history, or fate. These orientations are all impersonal. None of them justify a moral concern for the environment, or even for the rights of individual persons.

This explains why movements addressing pollution as well as other moral concerns have originated in the part of the world historically most influenced by Biblical thinking. And it explains why our scientific data and eyewitness reports of the worst forms of pollution now come from the Second and Third Worlds. In Eastern Europe, after seventy years of the impersonal utopian ideology of Marxist socialism, and in many areas of the Third World which have pursued indigenous religious and nationalistic goals rather than opening themselves to a more European view of human life, the destruction of man and earth has taken on enormous proportions.

Under socialism, the abolition of private property and of rewards for personal effort have not produced a protected earth. Chernobyl is but the tip of an iceberg. Sloppy workmanship, bureaucratic legalism, untrained decision-makers, the sacrifice of people in the name of a futuristic ideology, and the emphasis on equality have left behind an immense acreage of polluted earth, destroyed forests, undrinkable water, open sewers, and deposits of nuclear waste in open range lands.

Without an informed and critical public, with only the Party determining what is moral, and when no present sacrifice of integrity and health is to be spared for the achievement of the Socialist ideal, no effort could be set free, no mind and heart sensitized to pursue environmental concerns.

A similar observation can be made concerning another impersonal ideology, though it seems kinder and more humane. When nature is viewed as the will of God, when circumstances are animated by spirits, as in African tribal religions, human death and natural pollution are accepted as a just consequence of life itself. They are not to be objected to, for there is no outside court of appeals to which the objection can be addressed. Life itself is merely a repetition of what went before, a submission to fate.

Neither indigenous nature religions, nor awakening nationalisms, nor the scientific materialism in Marxist societies can show us a better, more sensitive, more humane and caring way. We are forced back to the dynamic of free, educated, concerned—albeit evil—people. Such people recognize the challenge of their natural environment, for better or for worse. They understand that they will reap what they sow. The only adequate basis for environmental activism was laid in the teachings of historic Judaism and Christianity. The Judeo-Christian tradition is not able to prevent its adherents from making mistakes in their treatment of the environment;

but it does furnish a basis for rational and valid criticism of those mistakes.

Many formerly convinced Socialists on both sides of the Iron Curtain have recognized the need for productive, creative, and therefore capitalistic societies. Only capitalism can afford making investments toward a protected earth for the sake of protecting human life.

Like converted Socialists, many from pagan backgrounds also wish to find ways of educating and liberating their people from the confines of an uncaring nature. They want to learn what makes people free and productive, creative and willing to address the needs of their neighbors. Often we fail to help such people see how much their own cultural, political, and social background is the root of the problem. But viability is not the result of nature left to itself, but of human effort to tackle problems.

Even within the framework of capitalism, of course, great foresight is necessary to foster both effort and restraint, both use and preservation, both consumption and restoration. To protect both man and nature requires a high view of human beings and of one's own descendants. They must become and remain indisposable. Solid and reliable laws, based on a comprehensive philosophy of life and not subject to democratic whims under short-term goals, must reflect this high and long-term perspective. Only in the Bible do we have a basis for such a high view of the worth of individual men and women.

Only the context of Biblical thinking sustains an outrage about, and a deliberate effort to solve, perceived problems. It is one of the deep ironies of our day that objections against a Biblical view of man are raised the loudest by those who daily benefit from the efforts they wish to abolish. They look for a kinder and more humane model and suggest to have seen it in a Socialist view of man, or in Eastern religion's denial of self.

They confront those who, after centuries of suffering, exploitation, religious and political bondage, and too much immaterial spirituality or ideological rhetoric, desire nothing more than a dry bed, enough food and health, and a future for their children. The first lot seeks a future that *breaks* with the present. The second seeks to break with the past simply to *have* a present.

The dream of socialism has been punctured. It cannot be sustained. It has no innocence after brutalizing millions for decades. Neither can pagan religions provide for human life. They give neither salvation nor life-support. Only the Bible has ever been able to provide both hope and present possibilities for human beings. The Bible teaches us that the very concern for life, including life threatened by a wasteful and exploitative use of nature, is a concern *for individual life now.* We care because, according to the Bible, the individual person matters. We produce more food, better health, broader education, wiser government, better-informed media, safer tools, and better laws because individual people matter. For that same reason we vote, discuss, warn, and preach. Neither socialism nor non-Christian religions have ever produced or embraced such concerns. Neither has delivered the good life for its citizens, not even an ecologically good one.

The Bible's story about Adam and Eve working, even against the sweat of the brow, to produce life for themselves and their children is the rightful response of people who care in a fallen world. They did not resign themselves, did not accept the status quo. They understood that their calling was to live. Dominion over the earth includes dominion over selfishness, exploitive attitudes, and false ideas. People cut down the groves Lynn White talks about because these trees were the focus of a hideous, inhuman, and deadly religious philosophy. They fought lies, because the truth was worth knowing.

The Bible speaks God's word against both human autonomy and resignation. It judges and calls for accountability, but it also encourages and calls for creative action. It speaks loudly against the materialism of modern man in his frivolous selfishness, lack of concern for future generations, and lack of understanding of the limits of nature. But it also bursts the limits imposed by those who see nature itself as the limit. To these, the Bible speaks of man's intellectual and moral ability to create resources, efficiency, and a pattern of responsibility which will free us from the fears of the naturalist and the resignation of the spiritualist.

Where the God of the Bible has informed the heart and mind of man, natural limits have been pushed back. God challenges our faculties. The Bible shows us that we are not sticks or stones in the wheel of history, but people made in God's image. Our history is not only filled with tragedies of human sin and shortsightedness—it is also a reflection of great efforts, both moral and technical, to *reject the limits*. Need produces not only moral guilt, but also a moral courage to overcome limits. Limits are not only warnings; they are also challenges. They provide evidence not only of human failings, but also of human abilities. Man is the greatest resource.

Obviously, believers in the God of the Bible have often failed to live up to their high calling as caretakers of God's creation. Much criticism of our

Western culture's handling of the environment is both valid and necessary. And where change has been produced, we are the better off for it. Waste is reduced; new resources are discovered and used. When that criticism is directed against the worship of things, the pursuit of personal affluence and security, it is well placed. But the criticism is not often enough raised against what is truly wrong in human actions. It is raised rather, as Schaeffer pointed out again and again, toward the philosophic foundation of the only truly humane society—toward the God of the Bible and His Word. Using wastefulness as the accusation, the verdict of the ecologist often does not call for restitution, but for the life of the Defendant. His existence, not his alleged crime, is judged. The problem will be solved by killing the accused!

Such suggestions can only come from polluted dreams of those who embrace visions of a pure nature more than work towards life-supporting efforts. A moral effort can only have the living person as a focus, not an uninhabited paradise. Where nature sets the terms for human existence, each person will be treated "naturally"; i.e., without respect for real needs arising out of life in a fallen world.

Man is called to creatively confront the results of a fallen world, not to abandon himself to those results. He can do this courageously when, rather than seeing himself as out of tune with an impersonal, uncaring "Mother Nature," he sees himself as being loved by the God in whose image he is made. Nature, no less than man, suffers under the tragic results of the Fall. That is why Adam had to plow against thorns and thistles in order to put food on the table. And that is why the Bible speaks of the need to live not only by bread, nuts, and berries, which nature might provide. Instead, every word from the mouth of God is to give direction, correction, and encouragement. That word tells us of iron under every mountain and copper under every hill to be used. That word alone tells us of a reality not readily apparent in the ebb and flow of time, the normality of being, the naturalness of birth and death.

That word is truth, life, and the only way to truly love our neighbor enough to put up a fight for his spiritual . . . and physical . . . survival. We must address his real needs and work towards substantial solutions for the sake of his life, even if it means changing the face of nature.

For the death of man can not only result from a polluted earth, but also, and much sooner, from the acceptance of a worldview which does not treasure the life of persons. For too long have millions been denied basic improvements in the human condition because of ways, faiths, and religions that reduce man to particles of a cosmic "one" and offer nothing but death. The Bible uniquely directs us to live.

Appendix A

The Historical Roots of Our Ecologic Crisis

Lynn White, Jr.

A conversation with Aldous Huxley not infrequently put one at the receiving end of an unforgettable monologue. About a year before his lamented death he was discoursing on a favorite topic: man's unnatural treatment of nature and its sad results. To illustrate his point he told how, during the previous summer, he had returned to a little valley in England where he had spent many happy months as a child. Once it had been composed of delightful grassy glades; now it was becoming overgrown with unsightly brush because the rabbits that formerly kept such growth under control had largely succumbed to a disease, myxomatosis, that was deliberately introduced by the local farmers to reduce the rabbits' destruction of crops. Being something of a Philistine, I could be silent no longer, even in the interest of great rhetoric. I interrupted to point out that the rabbit itself had been brought as a domestic animal to England in 1176, presumably to improve the protein diet of the peasantry.

All forms of life modify their contexts. The most spectacular and benign instance is doubtless the coral polyp. By serving its own ends, it has created a vast undersea world favorable to thousands of other kinds of animals and plants. Ever since man became a numerous species he has affected his environment notably. The hypothesis that his fire-drive method of hunting created the world's great grasslands and helped to exterminate the monster mammals of the Pleistocene from much of the globe is plausible, if not proved. For six millennia at least, the banks of the lower Nile have been a human artifact rather than the swampy African jungle which nature, apart from man, would have made it. The Aswan Dam, flooding 5,000 square miles, is only the latest stage in a long process. In many regions terracing or irrigation, overgrazing, the cutting of forests by Romans to build ships to fight Carthaginians or by Crusaders to solve the logistics problems of their expeditions have profoundly changed some ecologies. Observation that the French landscape falls into two basic types, the open fields of the north and the *bocage* of the south and west, inspired Marc Bloch to undertake his classic study of medieval agricultural methods. Quite unintentionally, changes in human ways often affect nonhuman nature. It has been noted, for example, that the advent of the automobile eliminated huge flocks of sparrows that once fed on the horse manure littering every street.

The history of ecologic change is still so rudimentary that we know little about what really happened, or what the results were. The extinction of the European aurochs as late as 1627 would seem to have been a simple case of overenthusiastic hunting. On more intricate matters it often is impossible to find solid information. For a thousand years or more the Frisians and Hollanders have been pushing back the North Sea, and the process is culminating in our own time in the reclamation of the Zuider Zee. What, if any, species of animals, birds, fish, shore life, or plants have died out in the process? In their epic combat with Neptune, have the Netherlanders overlooked ecological values in such a way that the quality of human life in the Netherlands has suffered? I cannot discover that the questions have ever been asked, much less answered.

People, then, have often been a dynamic element in their own environment, but in the present state of historical scholarship we usually do not know exactly when, where, or with what effects man-induced changes came. As we enter the last third of the twentieth century, however, concern for the problem of ecologic backlash is mounting feverishly. Natural science, conceived as the effort to understand the nature of things, had flourished in several eras and among several peoples. Similarly there had been an age-old accumulation of technological skills, sometimes growing rapidly, sometimes slowly. But it was not until about four generations ago that Western Europe and North America arranged a marriage between science and technology, a union of the theoretical and the empirical approaches to our natural environment. The emergence in widespread practice of the Baconian creed that scientific knowledge means technological power over nature can scarcely be dated before about 1850, save in the chemical industries, where it is anticipated in the eighteenth century. Its acceptance as a normal pattern of action may mark the greatest event in human history since the invention of agriculture, and perhaps in nonhuman terrestrial history as well.

Almost at once the new situation forced the

crystallization of the novel concept of ecology; indeed, the word *ecology* first appeared in the English language in 1873. Today, less than a century later, the impact of our race upon the environment has so increased in force that it has changed in essence. When the first cannons were fired, in the early fourteenth century, they affected ecology by sending workers scrambling to the forests and mountains for more potash, sulfur, iron ore, and charcoal, with some resulting erosion and defor-estation. Hydrogen bombs are of a different order: a war fought with them might alter the genetics of all life on this planet. By 1285 London had a smog problem arising from the burning of soft coal, but our present combustion of fossil fuels threatens to change the chemistry of the globe's atmosphere as a whole, with consequences which we are only begin-ning to guess. With the population explosion, the carcinoma of planless urbanism, the now geological deposits of sewage and garbage, surely no creature other than man has ever managed to foul its nest in such short order.

There are many calls to action, but specific pro-posals, however worthy as individual items, seem too partial, palliative, negative: ban the bomb, tear down the billboards, give the Hindus contraceptives and tell them to eat their sacred cows. The simplest solution to any suspect change is, of course, to stop it, or, better yet, to revert to a romanticized past: make those ugly gasoline stations look like Anne Hathaway's cottage or (in the Far West) like ghost-town saloons. The "wilderness area" mentality invariably advocates deep-freezing an ecology, whether San Gimignano or the High Sierra, as it was before the first Kleenex was dropped. But neither atavism nor prettification will cope with the ecologic crisis of our time.

What shall we do? No one yet knows. Unless we think about fundamentals, our specific measures may produce new backlashes more serious than those they are designed to remedy.

As a beginning we should try to clarify our thinking by looking, in some historical depth, at the presuppositions that underlie modern technology and science. Science was traditionally aristocratic, speculative, intellectual in intent; technology was lower-class, empirical, action-oriented. The quite sudden fusion of these two, towards the middle of the nineteenth century, is surely related to the slightly prior and contemporary democratic revolutions which, by reducing social barriers, tended to assert a functional unity of brain and hand. Our ecologic crisis is the product of an emerging, entirely novel, democratic culture. The issue is whether a democratized world can survive its own implications. Presumably we cannot unless we rethink our axioms.

THE WESTERN TRADITIONS OF TECHNOLOGY AND SCIENCE

One thing is so certain that it seems stupid to verbalize it: both modern technology and modern science are distinctively *Occidental*. Our technology has absorbed elements from all over the world, notably from China; yet everywhere today, whether in Japan or in Nigeria, successful technology is Western. Our science is the heir to all the sciences of the past, especially perhaps to the work of the great Islamic scientists of the Middle Ages, who so often outdid the ancient Greeks in skill and perspicacity: al-Razi in medicine, for example; or ibn-al-Haytham in optics; or Omar Khayyam in mathematics. Indeed, not a few works of such geniuses seem to have vanished in the original Arabic and to survive only in medieval Latin translations that helped to lay the foundations for later Western developments. Today, around the globe, all significant science is Western in style and method, whatever the pigmentation or language of the scientists.

A second pair of facts is less well recognized because they result from quite recent historical scholarship. The leadership of the West, both in technology and in science, is far older than the so-called Scientific Revolution of the seventeenth century or the so-called Industrial Revolution of the eighteenth century. These terms are in fact outmoded and obscure the true nature of what they try to describe—significant stages in two long and separate developments. By A.D. 1000 at the latest—and perhaps, feebly, as much as 200 years earlier—the West began to apply water power to industrial processes other than milling grain. This was followed in the late twelfth century by the harnessing of wind power. From simple beginnings, but with remarkable consistency of style, the West rapidly expanded its skills in the development of power machinery, labor-saving devices, and automation. Those who doubt should contemplate that most monumental achievement in the history of automation: the weight-driven mechanical clock, which appeared in two forms in the early fourteenth century. Not in craftsmanship but in basic technological capacity, the Latin West of the later Middle Ages far outstripped its elaborate, sophisticated, and aesthetically magnificent sister cultures, Byzantium and Islam. In 1444 a great Greek ecclesiastic, Bessarion, who had gone to Italy, wrote a letter to a prince in Greece. He is amazed by the superiority of Western ships, arms, textiles, glass. But above all he is astonished by the spectacle of waterwheels sawing timbers and pumping the bellows of blast furnaces. Clearly, he had seen nothing of the sort in the Near East.

By the end of the fifteenth century the technological superiority of Europe was such that its small, mutually hostile nations could spill out over all the rest of the world, conquering, looting, and colonizing. The symbol of this technological superiority is the fact that Portugal, one of the weakest states of the Occident, was able to become, and to remain for a century, mistress of the East Indies. And we must remember that the technology of Vasco da Gama and Albuquerque was built by pure empiricism, drawing remarkably little support or inspiration from science.

In the present-day vernacular understanding, modern science is supposed to have begun in 1543, when both Copernicus and Vesalius published their great works. It is not derogation of their accomplishments, however, to point out such structures as the *Fabrica* and the *De revolutionibus* do not appear overnight. The distinctive Western tradition of science, in fact, began in the late eleventh century with a massive movement of translation of Arabic and Greek scientific works into Latin. A few notable books—Theophrastus, for example—escaped the West's avid new appetite for science, but within less than 200 years effectively the entire corpus of Greek and Muslim science was available in Latin, and was being eagerly read and criticized in the new European universities. Out of criticism arose new observation, speculation, and increasing distrust of ancient authorities. By the late thirteenth century Europe had seized global scientific leadership from the faltering hands of Islam. It would be as absurd to deny the profound originality of Newton, Galileo, or Copernicus as to deny that of the fourteenth century scholastic scientists like Buridan or Oresme on whose work they built. Before the eleventh century, science scarcely existed in the Latin West, even in Roman times. From the eleventh century onward, the scientific sector of Occidental culture has increased in a steady crescendo.

Since both our technological and our scientific movements got their start, acquired their character, and achieved world dominance in the Middle Ages, it would seem that we cannot understand their nature or their present impact upon ecology without examining fundamental medieval assumptions and developments.

MEDIEVAL VIEW OF MAN AND NATURE

Until recently, agriculture has been the chief occupation even in "advanced" societies; hence, any change in methods of tillage has much importance. Early plows, drawn by two oxen, did not normally turn the sod but merely scratched it. Thus, cross-plowing was needed and fields tended to be squarish. In the fairly light soils and semiarid climates of the Near East and Mediterranean, this worked well. But such a plow was inappropriate to the wet climate and often sticky soils of northern Europe. By the latter part of the seventh century after Christ, however, following obscure beginnings, certain northern peasants were using an entirely new kind of plow, equipped with a vertical knife to cut the line of the furrow, a horizontal share to slice under the sod, and a moldboard to turn it over. The friction of this plow with the soil was so great that it normally required not two but eight oxen. It attacked the land with such violence that cross-plowing was not needed, and fields tended to be shaped in long strips.

In the days of the scratch-plow, fields were distributed generally in units capable of supporting a single family. Subsistence farming was the presupposition. But no peasant owned eight oxen: to use the new and more efficient plow, peasants pooled their oxen to form large plow-teams, originally receiving (it would appear) plowed strips in proportion to their contribution. Thus, distribution of land was based no longer on the needs of a family but, rather, on the capacity of a power machine to till the earth. Man's relation to the soil was profoundly changed. Formerly man had been part of nature; now he was the exploiter of nature. Nowhere else in the world did farmers develop any analogous agricultural implement. Is it coincidence that modern technology, with its ruthlessness toward nature, has so largely been produced by descendants of these peasants of northern Europe?

This same exploitive attitude appears slightly before A.D. 830 in Western illustrated calendars. In older calendars the months were shown as passive personifications. The new Frankish calendars, which set the style for the Middle Ages, are very different: they show men coercing the world around them—plowing, harvesting, chopping trees, butchering pigs. Man and nature are two things, and man is master.

These novelties seem to be in harmony with larger intellectual patterns. What people do about their ecology depends on what they think about themselves in relation to things around them. Human ecology is deeply conditioned by beliefs about our nature and destiny—that is, by religion. To Western eyes this is very evident in, say, India or Ceylon. It is equally true of ourselves and of our medieval ancestors.

The victory of Christianity over paganism was the greatest psychic revolution in the history of our culture. It has become fashionable today to say that, for better or worse, we live in "the post-Christian age." Certainly the forms of our thinking and language have largely ceased to be Christian, but to my eye the substance often remains amazingly akin to that of the past. Our daily habits of action, for example, are dominated by an implicit faith in perpetual progress which was unknown either to Greco-Roman antiquity or to the Orient. It is rooted in, and is indefensible apart from, Judeo-Christian teleology. The fact that Communists share it merely helps to show what can be demonstrated on many other grounds: that Marxism, like Islam, is a Judeo-Christian heresy. We continue today to live, as we have lived for about 1,700 years, very largely in a context of Christian axioms.

What did Christianity tell people about their relations with the environment?

While many of the world's mythologies provide stories of creation, Greco-Roman mythology was singularly incoherent in this respect. Like Aristotle, the intellectuals of the ancient West denied that the visible world had had a beginning. Indeed, the idea of a beginning was impossible in the framework of their cyclical notion of time. In sharp contrast, Christianity inherited from Judaism not only a concept of time as nonrepetitive and linear but also a striking story of creation. By gradual stages a loving and all-powerful God had created light and darkness, the heavenly bodies, the earth and all its plants, animals, birds, and fishes. Finally, God had created Adam and, as an afterthought, Eve to keep man from being lonely. Man named all the animals, thus establishing his dominance over them. God planned all of this explicitly for man's benefit and rule: no item in the physical creation had any purpose save to serve man's purposes. And, although man's body is made of clay, he is not simply part of nature: he is made in God's image.

Especially in its Western form, Christianity is the most anthropocentric religion the world has seen. As early as the second century both Tertullian and Saint Irenaeus of Lyons were insisting that when God shaped Adam he was foreshadowing the image of the incarnate Christ, the Second Adam. Man shares, in great measure, God's transcendence of nature. Christianity, in absolute contrast to ancient paganism and Asia's religions (except, perhaps, Zoroastrianism), not only established a dualism of man and nature, but also insisted that it is God's will that man exploit nature for his proper ends.

At the level of the common people this worked out in an interesting way. In Antiquity every tree, every spring, every stream, every hill had its own *genius loci*, its guardian spirit. These spirits were accessible to men, but were very unlike men; centaurs, fauns, and mermaids show their ambivalence. Before one cut a tree, mined a mountain, or dammed a brook, it was important to placate the spirit in charge of that particular situation, and to keep it placated. By destroying pagan animism, Christianity made it possible to exploit nature in a mood of indifference to the feelings of natural objects.

It is often said that for animism the Church substituted the cult of saints. True; but the cult of saints is functionally quite different from animism. The saint is not *in* natural objects; he may have special shrines, but his citizenship is in heaven.

Moreover, a saint is entirely a man; he can be approached in human terms. In addition to saints, Christianity of course also had angels and demons inherited from Judaism and perhaps, at one remove, from Zoroastrianism. But these were all as mobile as the saints themselves. The spirits in natural objects, which formerly had protected nature from man, evaporated. Man's effective monopoly on spirit in this world was confirmed, and the old inhibitions to the exploitation of nature crumbled.

When one speaks in such sweeping terms, a note of caution is in order. Christianity is a complex faith, and its consequences differ in differing contexts. What I have said may well apply to the medieval West, where in fact technology made spectacular advances. But the Greek East, a highly civilized realm of equal Christian devotion, seems to have produced no marked technological innovation after the late seventh century, when Greek fire was invented. The key to the contrast may perhaps be found in a difference in the tonality of piety and thought which students of comparative theology find between the Greek and the Latin Churches. The Greeks believed that sin was intellectual blindness, and that salvation was found in illumination, orthodoxy—that is, clear thinking. The Latins, on the other hand, felt that sin was moral evil, and that salvation was to be found in right conduct. Eastern theology has been intellectualist. Western theology has been voluntarist. The Greek saint contemplates; the Western saint acts. The implications of Christianity for the conquest of nature would emerge more easily in the Western atmosphere.

The Christian dogma of creation, which is found in the first clause of all the Creeds, has another meaning for our comprehension of today's ecologic crisis. By revelation, God had given man the Bible, the Book of Scripture. But since God had made nature, nature also must reveal the divine mentality. The religious study of nature for the better understanding of God was known as natural theology. In the early Church, and always in the Greek East, nature was conceived primarily as a symbolic system through which God speaks to men: the ant is a sermon to sluggards; rising flames are the symbol of the soul's aspiration. This view of nature was essentially artistic rather than scientific. While Byzantium preserved and copied great numbers of ancient Greek scientific texts, science as we conceive it could scarcely flourish in such an ambience.

However, in the Latin West by the early thirteenth century natural theology was following a very different bent. It was ceasing to be the decoding of the physical symbols of God's communication with man and was becoming the effort to understand God's mind by discovering how His creation operates. The rainbow was no longer simply a symbol of hope first sent to Noah after the Deluge: Robert Grosseteste, Friar Roger Bacon, and Theodoric of Freiberg produced startlingly sophisticated works on the optics of the rainbow, but they did it as a venture in religious understanding. From the thirteenth century onward, up to and including Leibnitz and Newton, every major scientist, in effect, explained his motivations in religious terms. Indeed, if Galileo had not been so expert an amateur theologian he would have got into far less trouble: the professionals resented his intrusion. And Newton seems to have regarded himself more as a theologian than as a scientist. It was not until the late eighteenth century that the hypothesis of God became unnecessary to many scientists.

It is often hard for the historian to judge, when men explain why they are doing what they want to do, whether they are offering real reasons or merely culturally acceptable reasons. The consistency with which scientists during the long formative centuries of Western science said that the task and the reward of the scientist was "to think God's thoughts after him" leads one to believe that this was their real motivation. If so, then modern Western science was cast in a matrix of Christian theology. The dynamism of religious devotion, shaped by the Judeo-Christian dogma of creation, gave it impetus.

AN ALTERNATIVE CHRISTIAN VIEW

We would seem to be headed toward conclusions unpalatable to many Christians. Since both *science* and *technology* are blessed words in our contemporary vocabulary, some may be happy at the notions, first, that, viewed historically, modern science is an extrapolation of natural theology and, second, that modern technology is at least partly to be explained as an Occidental, voluntarist realization of the Christian dogma of man's transcendence of, and rightful mastery over, nature. But, as we now recognize, somewhat over a century ago science and technology—hitherto quite separate activities—joined to give mankind powers which, to judge by many of the ecologic effects, are out of control. If so, Christianity bears a huge burden of guilt.

I personally doubt that disastrous ecologic backlash can be avoided simply by applying to our problems more science and more technology. Our science and technology have grown out of Christian attitudes toward man's relation to nature which are almost universally held not only by Christians and neo-Christians but also by those who fondly regard themselves as post-Christians. Despite Copernicus, all the cosmos rotates around our little globe. Despite Darwin, we are not, in our hearts, part of the natural process. We are superior to nature, contemptuous of it, willing to use it for our slightest whim. The newly elected Governor of California, like myself a churchman but less troubled than I, spoke for the Christian tradition when he said (as is alleged), "when you've seen one redwood tree, you've seen them all." To a Christian a tree can be no more than a physical fact. The whole concept of the sacred grove is alien to Christianity and to the ethos of the West. For nearly two millennia Christian missionaries have been chopping down sacred groves, which are idolatrous because they assume spirit in nature.

What we do about ecology depends on our ideas of the man-nature relationship. More science and more technology are not going to get us out of the present ecologic crisis until we find a new religion, or rethink our old one. The beatniks, who are the basic revolutionaries of our time, show a sound instinct in their affinity for Zen Buddhism, which conceives of the man-nature relationship as very nearly the mirror image of the Christian view. Zen, however, is as deeply conditioned by Asian history as Christianity is by the experience of the West, and I am dubious of its viability among us.

Possibly we should ponder the greatest radical in Christian history since Christ: Saint Francis of Assisi. The prime miracle of Saint Francis is the fact that he did not end at the stake, as many of his left-wing followers did. He was so clearly heretical that a General of the Franciscan Order, Saint Bonaventura, a great and perceptive Christian, tried to suppress the early accounts of Franciscanism. The key to an understanding of Francis is his belief in the virtue of humility—not merely for the individual but for man as a species. Francis tried to depose man from his monarchy over creation and set up a democracy of all God's creatures. With him the ant is no longer simply a homily for the lazy, flames a sign of the thrust of the soul toward union with God; now they are Brother Ant and Sister Fire, praising the Creator in their own ways as Brother Man does in his.

Later commentators have said that Francis preached to the birds as a rebuke to men who would not listen. The records do not read so: he urged the little birds to praise God, and in spiritual ecstasy they flapped their wings and chirped rejoicing. Legends of saints, especially the Irish saints, had long told of their dealings with animals but always,

I believe, to show their human dominance over creatures. With Francis it is different. The land around Gubbio in the Apennines was being ravaged by a fierce wolf. Saint Francis, says the legend, talked to the wolf and persuaded him of the error of his ways. The wolf repented, died in the odor of sanctity, and was buried in consecrated ground.

What Sir Steven Runciman calls "the Franciscan doctrine of the animal soul" was quickly stamped out. Quite possibly it was in part inspired, consciously or unconsciously, by the belief in reincarnation held by the Cathar heretics who at that time teemed in Italy and southern France, and who presumably had got it originally from India. It is significant that at just the same moment, about 1200, traces of metempsychosis are found also in western Judaism, in the Provencal *Cabbala*. But Francis held neither to transmigration of souls nor to pantheism. His view of nature and of man rested on a unique sort of pan-psychism of all things animate and inanimate, designed for the glorification of their transcendent Creator, who, in the ultimate gesture of cosmic humility, assumed flesh, lay helpless in a manger, and hung dying on a scaffold.

I am not suggesting that many contemporary Americans who are concerned about our ecologic crisis will be either able or willing to counsel with wolves or exhort birds. However, the present increasing disruption of the global environment is the product of a dynamic technology and science which were originating in the Western medieval world against which Saint Francis was rebelling in so original a way. Their growth cannot be understood historically apart from distinctive attitudes toward nature which are deeply grounded in Christian dogma. The fact that most people do not think of these attitudes as Christian is irrelevant. No new set of basic values has been accepted in our society to displace those of Christianity. Hence we shall continue to have a worsening ecologic crisis until we reject the Christian axiom that nature has no reason for existence save to serve man.

The greatest spiritual revolutionary in Western history, Saint Francis, proposed what he thought was an alternative Christian view of nature and man's relation to it: he tried to substitute the idea of the equality of all creatures, including man, for the idea of man's limitless rule of creation. He failed. Both our present science and our present technology are so tinctured with orthodox Christian arrogance toward nature that no solution for our ecologic crisis can be expected from them alone. Since the roots of our trouble are so largely religious, the remedy must also be essentially religious, whether we call it that or not. We must rethink and refeel our nature and destiny. The profoundly religious, but heretical, sense of the primitive Franciscans for the spiritual autonomy of all parts of nature may point a direction. I propose Francis as a patron saint for ecologists.

Appendix B

Why Worry About Nature?

Richard L. Means

Albert Schweitzer once wrote, "The great fault of all ethics hitherto has been that they believed themselves to have to deal only with the relation of man to man." Modern ethical discussion does not seem to have removed itself very far from this fallacy. Joseph Fletcher's *Situation Ethics: The New Morality*, for instance, deals piecemeal with man's relations to his fellows without even suggesting that man's relation to nature—to the physical and biological world—raises questions of moral behavior. Perhaps this oversight is due to the general psychological and subjective tone of much current social criticism. Or, even more likely, it represents the "revolt against formalism," the eschewing of the abstract and sweeping interpretations of man and nature once the passion of American social scientists.

It is true that the Thoreau-like comments of Joseph Wood Krutch or the aggressive naturalistic interpretations of the Austrian scientist, Konrad Lorenz, find a grudging response among some social scientists. But contemporary social scientists have so completely separated conditions of culture from nature that it will take some intellectual effort to overcome this dichotomy. Moreover, although the relations of man and nature may be envisioned in various ways—all the way from control to passive obedience—the notion that man's relation to nature is a moral one finds very few articulate champions, even among contemporary religious writers. Harvey Cox's book, *The Secular City*, for example, is set in an urban world in rather extreme isolation from the surrounding problems of resources, food, disease, etc. The city is taken for granted and the moral dimensions of Cox's analysis are limited to man's relations to man within this urban world, and not with the animals, the plants, the trees, the air—that is, the natural habitat.

Eric Hoffer, one of the few contemporary social critics who have met head-on the issue of man's relationship to nature, has warned in these pages of the danger of romanticizing nature. ["A

Strategy for the War with Nature," *SR*, February 5, 1966.] Longshoreman, dishwasher, student of human tragedy, and exposer of the corruptions and perversions of power, Mr. Hoffer says that the great accomplishment of man is to transcend nature, to separate one's self from the demands of instinct. Thus, according to Hoffer, a fundamental characteristic of man is to be found in his capacity to free himself from the restrictions of the physical and biological.

In a way, Hoffer is correct. Surely the effects on man of flood, famine, fire, and earthquake have been great and hardly indicate a beneficence in nature which is ready and willing to rush headlong to the succor of man. But Hoffer's attack is basically political. It is an attack on "romantic individualism"—a special interpretation of man's relation to nature. Hoffer knows full well that romantic individualism leads easily to a kind of egoism and antirationalism which can pervert and destroy democratic institutions.

One is reminded of Hitler's call to neglect reason and to "think with one's blood." Values—tradition, home soil, nationalism, and race—have often been legitimized on the basis of a vague nature mysticism. Such a nature mysticism is the very essence of romantic individualism (though, of course, there may be other types of nature romanticism which do not advocate egotist striving). Perhaps the problem lies in the focus on the "individual" as delineated by Hoffer. He assumes that the response to nature couched in the terms of a naive faith in nature's bountiful, miracle-working properties is an individual response. And, of course, it always is, to a degree, but, by failure to consider the collective or social side of man's relation to nature, the true moral dimensions of the problem are obscured.

It may be that *man* is at war with nature, but *men* are not (or, at least, cannot be). The reason is that certain individual attitudes and actions, when taken collectively, have consequences for nature, and these consequences may be most clearly understood under the stark realities of social survival itself. Take the problems of radioactive wastes, Strontium 90 contamination, etc. Man does not just do battle with the natural world; he may, in the act of cooperating with it, also shape and change it. Men join in a chain of decisions which facilitate the emergence of a new symbiotic relationship to nature— that is, we create civilization and culture. This crucial assumption strikes at the very roots of romantic individualism. One man, totally alone, acting before nature and using nature to satisfy needs of warmth, comfort, and creativity, is very difficult to imagine. Even Robinson Crusoe had his man Friday!

Hoffer seems to neglect the possibility that man's cooperation in the subjection of nature need not be conceptualized simply on the basis of brute force. Physical work, mechanical and otherwise—from the labor of the Chinese masses to the works of a sophisticated high-tower steeplejack—depends on the intrusion of human ideas into the natural world. Aided by machines, cranes, bulldozers, factories, transportation systems, computers, and laboratories, man does force nature's hand. This does not, however, force us to acceptance of metaphysical materialism, the naive belief that matter and physical force are the only realities. The power of ideas, of values, provides the presuppositions which in the first place create a particular web of human interaction between nature and man. The power of the contemplative idea, the chain of speculative reason, the mathematician's art, and the philosopher's dreams must also be considered. If this point of view is accepted, then the question of man's relation to nature is a much more crucial moral issue than Eric Hoffer seems to suggest.

What, then, is the moral crisis? It is, I think, a pragmatic problem—that is, it involves the actual social consequences of myriad and unconnected acts. The crisis comes from the combined results of a mistreatment of our environment. It involves the negligence of a small businessman on the Kalamazoo River, the irresponsibility of a large corporation on Lake Erie, the impatient use of insecticides by a farmer in California, the stripping of land by Kentucky mine operators. Unfortunately, there is a long history of unnecessary and tragic destruction of animal and natural resources on the face of this continent.

One might begin the indictment with the classical case of the passenger pigeon which once flew across America in tremendous numbers, and then end with the destruction of the seal industry. The trouble is, however, we do not seem to learn very much from these sad happenings, for (to the anguish of men who have thrilled to the images created by Herman Melville and the great white whale) such marine scientists as Scott McVay believe that commercial fishing is endangering the whale, the last abundant species in the world. For those more inclined toward a cash nexus, there goes a profitable industry. For those of us who have a respect for nature—in particular, for our mammalian kinsmen—the death of these great creatures will leave a void in God's creation and in the imagination of men for generations to come.

Another case in point is the attempt to dam and flood mile after mile of the Grand Canyon in order to produce more electricity—a commodity we seem to have in great abundance. The Grand Canyon, of course, is not a commodity; it is truly, in popular parlance, a "happening." Uncontrolled by man, created by nature, it cannot be duplicated. Any assault on its natural state is an equal attack on man's capacity to wonder, to contemplate his environment and nature's work. In short, such activities seem to belittle and diminish man himself. Thus the activities of those who suggest such destruction assume a restricted view of man and his capacity for joy in nature. In this sense, such activities are immoral. We could lengthen the list, but it should be clear that destruction of nature by man's gratuitous "busyness" and technological arrogance is the result of a thoughtless and mindless human activity.

A second basic issue is the growing biological pollution of the environment. Discussions of the pollution in just one river, the mighty Hudson, in financial terms stagger the imagination. The economic costs just to keep the river in its present undesirable state are immense—and to make any progress back toward a less polluted river will cost billions of dollars. The same is true of other great bodies of water.

And consider the state of the air we breathe. Air pollution has demonstrable ill effects on man, as many reports confirm. But in addition, for the economically minded, A. J. Haagen-Smit, a leading expert on air pollution, notes that a largely ignored breakdown in standards of efficiency and technology also is involved:

> From all the emissions of an automobile, the total loss of fuel energy is about 15 percent; in the U.S. that represents a loss of about $3 billion annually. It is remarkable that the automobile industry, which has a reputation for efficiency, allows such fuel waste.

Perhaps an issue becomes most moral when it is personal, existential—appeals to our own experience. Scientists vary in estimates of the time when the Great Lakes will be largely polluted, but the day of reckoning may be much too near. When I was a boy in Toledo, Ohio, summer after summer many of my neighbors and playmates went to cottages along the shores of Lake Erie. Today, visiting these cottages is anything but a happy event, and some owners are attempting desperately to sell their properties to any bidder. An analysis by Charles F. Powers and Andrew Robertson on "The Aging Great Lakes"

[*Scientific American,* November 1966] is not at all comforting for those of us who love the miles of sandy beach of Lake Michigan or the rugged, cold, wind-whipped shores of Lake Superior. Although Lake Michigan will not immediately turn into a polluted wasteland like Lake Erie, with dark spots of water without aeration where only worms can live, pollution is growing in the southern end of Lake Michigan. And these problems, as Powers and Robertson point out, are beginning to touch even relatively unspoiled Lake Superior.

Why is man's relation to nature a moral crisis? It is a moral crisis because it is a historical one involving man's history and culture, expressed at its roots by our religious and ethical views of nature—which have been relatively unquestioned in this context. The historian of medieval culture, Lynn White, Jr., brilliantly traced the origin and consequences of this expression in an insightful article in *Science* last March: "The Historical Roots of Our Ecologic Crisis." He argues that the Christian notion of a transcendent God, removed from nature and breaking into nature only through revelation, removed spirit from nature and allows, in the ideological sense, for an easy exploitation of nature.

On the American scene, the Calvinistic and the deistic concepts of God were peculiarly alike at this point. Both envisioned God as absolutely transcendent, apart from the world, isolated from nature and organic life. As to the contemporary implications of this dichotomy between spirit and nature, Professor White says:

> The newly elected Governor of California, like myself a churchman but less troubled than I, spoke for the Christian tradition when he said (as is alleged), "When you've seen one redwood tree, you've seen them all." To a Christian a tree can be no more than a physical fact. The whole concept of the sacred grove is alien to Christianity and to the ethos of the West. For nearly two millennia Christian missionaries have been chopping down sacred groves, which are idolatrous because they assume spirit in nature.

Perhaps, as Lynn White suggests, the persistence of this as a moral problem is illustrated in the protest of the contemporary generation of beats and hippies. Although the kind of "cool cat" aloofness expressed by this generation grates on the nerves of many of us, and more than a few "squares" find difficulty in "digging" the new hair styles (not to mention Twiggy), there may be a "sound instinct" involved in the fact that some of these so-called beats have turned to Zen Buddhism. It may represent an overdue perception of the fact that we need to appreciate more fully the religious and moral dimensions of the relation between nature and the human spirit.

Why do almost all of our wisest and most exciting social critics meticulously avoid the moral implications of this issue? Perhaps, in the name of political realism, it is too easy to fear the charge that one anthropomorphizes or spiritualizes nature. On the other hand, the refusal to connect the human spirit to nature may reflect the traditional thought pattern of Western society wherein nature is conceived to be a separate substance—a material—mechanical, and, in a metaphysical sense, irrelevant to man.

It seems to me much more fruitful to think of nature as part of a system of human organization—as a variable, a changing condition—which interacts with man and culture. If nature is so perceived, then a love, a sense of awe, and a feeling of empathy with nature need not degenerate into a subjective, emotional bid for romantic individualism. On the contrary, such a view should help destroy egoistic, status politics, for it helps unmask the fact that other men's activities are not just private, inconsequential, and limited in themselves; their arts, mediated through changes in nature, affect my life, my children, and the generations to come. In this sense, justification of a technological arrogance toward nature on the basis of dividends and profits is not just bad economics—it is basically an immoral act. And our contemporary moral crisis, then, goes much deeper than questions of political power and law, of urban riots and slums. It may, at least in part, reflect American society's almost utter disregard for the value of nature.

Notes

CHAPTER ONE: *"What Have They Done to Our Fair Sister?"*

1. For a technical study of Wingate's work, see *Science* magazine, March 1, 1969, pp. 979-981.
2. From "Strange Days" by the Doors, Elektra EKS 74014. Copyright Polydon Records Ltd.
3. This appears as Appendix A of this book.
4. See Appendix B.

CHAPTER TWO: *Pantheism: Man Is No More Than the Grass*

1. Aldous Huxley, *Island* (New York: Harper and Row, 1962; London: Penguin, n.d.), pp. 219, 220.
2. See "Wilful Waste, Woeful Want," by Max Kirschner, *The Listener,* January 26, 1967.

CHAPTER THREE: *Other Inadequate Answers*

1. For a detailed consideration of these points, only touched upon here, see the book *The God Who Is There* and *Escape from Reason.*
2. For a detailed consideration of these points, only touched upon here, see the book *The God Who Is There* and *Escape from Reason.*